The Shy Person's Guide to Love and Loving

Eric Weber and Judi Miller
with Allan Ishac

Times
BOOKS

Published by TIMES BOOKS, a division
of Quadrangle/The New York Times Book Co., Inc.
Three Park Avenue, New York, N.Y. 10016

Published simultaneously in Canada by
Fitzhenry & Whiteside, Ltd., Toronto

Library of Congress Cataloging in Publication Data

Weber, Eric, 1942-
The shy person's guide to love and loving.

1. Bashfulness. 2. Love
I. Miller, Judi, joint author.
II. Title.
BF575.B3W38   1979   158'.2   79-51438
ISBN 0-8129-0845-7

Manufactured in the United States of America

Acknowledgments

We would like to thank the many people whose advice and suggestions during the writing of this book were invaluable, especially Dr. Robert Glick, Dr. Samuel Perry, Dr. Thomas Schreiber, and Renee Saltoun.

Contents

The Shy Person's Guide to Love and Loving

Introduction

SEVENTEEN YEARS ago we knew a young man who was so shy he often didn't go out for months at a time. One year, his sophomore year in college, he had a grand total of only three dates. And one of those was a blind date set up by a kindly friend of the young man's brother.

Sometimes, on those rare occasions when the young man was able to muster the courage to leave his room, he would visit singles bars. But do you know that during eight full months of frequenting some of the liveliest meeting places on Manhattan's upper East Side, the fellow approached only one woman. And she was a poor, forlorn-looking lass with a ravaged complexion and an expression so meek and pitiful the boy sensed she would consent to talk to anyone—even someone as unattractive and unworthy as himself. Yet when they lapsed into silence after only five minutes of conversation, the boy took it as a sign that the girl wasn't responding to him; and he fled her side and the bar and returned to his room and his dear companion, the RCA television set his parents had bought him for his high school graduation. For two full years he was unable to bring himself to enter a singles bar again.

Now let's flash forward seventeen years to the present. The shy young man in question is no longer so young; in fact, at thirty-six he is embarking on middle age. His hair has grown a little gray and his waistline has expanded an inch or two. But those changes are miniscule, mere window dressing compared to the truly major alteration that our hero has undergone in his personality. For now, nearly two decades later, the man isn't shy at all.

Wait a second, let us correct that. Perhaps he still is shy. Perhaps shyness is a trait, an ingredient of personality, that one never really sheds or leaves behind. And maybe this is good. Darwin wrote of an animal's instinct for self-preservation. Perhaps on one level shyness is actually a self-protective mechanism that keeps people from exposing themselves to danger. For example, shyness or reticence often helps people pace themselves into a relationship, thus preventing entanglement in a troublesome or undesirable affair.

The tragedy of shyness, however, is when it keeps a shy person from experiencing *any* social interaction, when it prevents him or her from having a happy, healthy, participatory love life.

Well, then, if the man described above still is shy, how exactly has he changed? The answer is that he no longer *acts* shy, no longer lives a shy person's lifestyle. Even if he still is shy on the inside, given to occasional bouts of insecurity, self-dislike, and feelings of unworthiness, his outward behavior is outgoing, social, assertive, and confident. And that is all that really matters. When you're meeting people for the first time, they do not respond to what is lurking in your heart, to the fears and doubts harbored in your mind. They respond, in the main, to the outer you, to the face and posture you present to the world. The inner you may be pathetically shy, but if the outer you appears engaging, inviting, and *interested*, people will respond in kind. Look what this style of behavior has done for our hero.

Today, at thirty-six, he is married to a thoughtful, charming, and extraordinarily attractive woman. He is the father of four children, the president of his own publishing company, and has even become a bit of a celebrity on television and radio talk shows. Part of his life story was just dramatized on a two-hour made-for-TV-movie on ABC. Merv Griffin based an entire show around one of his books. The man has worked with well-known people like Fran Tarkenton, Pearl Bailey, Ernest Gallo, John Wayne, and Alan King, and he has even become good friends with some of them. All this from a fellow who, when he was a nineteen-year-old college sophomore, was so self-conscious, so afraid to approach other people, he often holed up in his room for months at a time.

In case you haven't guessed by now, the man we're talking about is Eric Weber, one of the authors of this book. And the reason we're carrying on so about what has happened to him is not that he's so proud, he's *amazed!* At one time in his life he wouldn't have dared to approach a strange girl on a bus or in a museum. Yet by the time Eric was twenty-five he thought nothing of walking up to a glamorous Swedish model in his local bistro to ask if he might join her at her table.

At this point we're sure you're probably thinking, *Well, that's fine for Eric. So things have worked out okay in his life. But what about me? How am I going to change? What's the secret for conquering shyness? And will it work for me?*

The secret, quite simply, is this: You have to learn how to stop acting shy. You have to learn how to start acting unshy. That, in a nutshell, is how the authors of this book have conquered their shyness. And how you, in less than one month, can conquer yours.

Now, before you begin complaining that you didn't shell out money for a book only to be told the way to get over your shyness is to stop acting shy, let us tell you a story.

When Eric was deep in the pits of his shyness, virtually

suffocating from it, he tried just about *everything* he could to get over it. He read books on winning friends and influencing people. He studied yoga and dabbled in self-analysis, read psychology books and books on the power of positive thinking. He attended lectures on self-awareness and took courses in the latest methods of achieving total self-discovery and self-fulfill-ment. None of it, not one bit of it, helped. Occasionally Eric would get stoked up and storm out to the nearest discotheque or singles bar. But the moment he got close enough to hear the music booming through the door, every last milligram of his self-confidence would disappear as if by magic. He'd stand around looking at the crowd knowing in his bones that there was no way in the world that he was ever going to meet anyone. So after five or ten minutes of self-conscious agony he would head back home.

Why then weren't any of these self-help books or programs working for him? According to their advertisements they had helped millions find their way to a happy, successful life. Why was Eric finding their teachings so thin, so unmotivating, so ineffectual? The answer is that every one of them is based on a tenet that doesn't make any sense at all: Before Others Can Love You, You Have to Learn to Love Yourself. This seems to be the foundation of just about every self-help system we've come across.

When Eric was nineteen years old, he *couldn't* learn to love himself. Most of the time he hated the way he looked, hated the way he talked, and often thought he was boring and dumb and inconsequential. It just wasn't possible for him to *learn* to like himself. And no amount of chanting or pretending or telling himself that he was handsome and pleasant and scintillating could convince him that he was lovable. Since he couldn't master the most basic technique of any of the self-help programs with which he was dabbling, he found the entire systems to be of little use.

So what finally got Eric over the edge? What single, momentous event helped him begin to conquer shyness and grope his way toward a more active, fun-filled social life? As usually happens with the great apocalypses of our lives, he didn't recognize this one until years after it occurred. But nevertheless, it did occur. And as we look back on it we can clearly see it marked the beginning of a whole new way in which Eric began relating to members of the opposite sex.

Here's what happened. One spring evening during his twentieth year, a friend unexpectedly dropped by to see if Eric wanted to go into Manhattan to have a few beers at the West End Tavern across from Columbia University. Because Eric wasn't anticipating an evening out on the town, he was lounging around the house in an old, torn pair of jeans. He hadn't shaved in several days, nor had he washed his hair that morning, an absolutely necessary procedure for his combing it the way he liked best. In short, he looked grubby and messy, just like you might expect any college student to look who thought he was going to be sitting around in front of the tube all evening.

Now perhaps a more outgoing young man wouldn't have been so threatened by the notion of heading out for a beer looking like such a slob. But to Eric the idea was nothing short of suicidal. "Can't go," he told his friend Bud. "I haven't even showered and shaved."

"So what?" Bud said incredulously. Neither had he. Why make such a big production out of going out for a few brews?

Desperately Eric tried to wriggle out of going, but Bud just wasn't accepting any excuses. It is almost impossible to describe the trepidation and gloom and panic Eric felt descend upon him as he headed out to Bud's car. Bud was handsome. Eric knew that he was not. Bud was outgoing, Eric was not. Bud was fearless; he would approach any woman who caught his eye without a second thought. Eric could hardly get himself to approach anyone. And on those rare occasions when he did, it was certainly never with any real spontaniety. His style was wooden, stiff, jerky, and not exactly ideal for fun-loving college students in a fun-loving college bar.

As they drove down the Westside Highway, Eric imagined

that Bud would meet a beautiful, impulsive drama student, and that he himself would come up empty-handed. He pictured Bud and his newfound paramour driving Eric home late at night, dropping him off at the bottom of his driveway, and watching with pity as he trudged slowly toward the front door, a beaten man, a loser. *God!*

The instant the two young men stepped into the West End Tavern, Eric's terror grew even greater. The place was crowded with sexy, good-looking students, smiling at each other, ogling each other, and sweet-talking each other. Eric positioned himself a few feet away from the bar as his friend waded right through the crowd to order their beers. *Clearly this is not the place for me,* Eric decided. The bar was too fast, too sex-charged, too avant-garde. Eric made up his mind that he would simply chug down his beer and then tell Bud he had to go back and study for an economics exam, even if it meant taking the subway uptown and the bus home by himself. That made him feel a little better. He had a plan now, a method of escape.

Bud soon returned and the two young men stood there for a minute sipping their beers silently and looking around at the girls. Bud's face was eager and optimistic, Eric's was wide-eyed with fear. *Still,* he thought with comfort, *I have my plan.* Fortunately for Eric, he never had time to put it into action. About halfway through his beer, Bud suddenly grabbed Eric's arm and began pulling him toward the bar. "Those two," he whispered. "They're terrific!" Indeed they were. Sitting on bar stools directly in front of the boys were two young women. One was tall and lanky with black medium-length hair and a pale angelic face. Her friend was shorter with long golden locks and a heartshaped visage dominated by enormous blue eyes. Eric felt an insane impulse to flee. This was a kamikaze mission they were on, and even if Bud weren't destined to be shot down, Eric knew more surely than he knew anything that he would be lucky to walk out of the West End alive, much less with one of these two spectacular women by his side. He considered turning on his heels and dashing from the bar, but the die was cast, the two men were hurtling forward, and there was no turning back.

"Hi," Bud said with a pleasant grin. "This is my friend, Eric. I'm Bud. How're you doing?" Eric was absolutely convinced that the girls were going to signal the bartender to have them removed, or at the very least turn their backs and cold-shoulder them for eternity. But to his amazement, the girls simply smiled back and introduced themselves. Eric can't remember the dark-haired girl's name, but her friend was Suzy and she smiled at him so warmly and pleasantly he thought she must have been from one of those devoutly religious families in which the parents are always drumming it into the kids' heads that they must be polite to *everybody* . . . even someone as goofy and unappealing as himself. *She probably feels sorry for me,* he concluded, *and doesn't want me to feel bad even though secretly she's got her eye on Bud.* He turned away from her to gaze around at the crowd so that she wouldn't have to feel obligated to go on smiling at him.

As Bud rattled on with the usual patter of small talk—Where are you from? Where do you go to school? (in their case, they were studying music and dance at Julliard)—Eric once again began plotting how to escape. He couldn't stand the pressure of the situation. Obviously both of these girls were falling for Bud. Better to get the hell out now rather than face the ignominy of watching them battle for his friend as he stood there unloved and alone. He began to feel so unhappy and dejected that he actually sensed himself growing faint. His face felt cold and his head light, and then, without quite knowing how it happened, he dropped his bottle of beer. Crash! It broke into hundreds of shards on the sawdust-covered floor. The whole bar erupted in a mighty cheer.

Eric was so embarrassed he could barely bring himself to look up at his group of friends. He felt an impulse to burrow under the sawdust and hide forever. But when he finally got the courage to meet his companions' eyes, he saw that they were all smiling at him . . . and not without a trace of admiration, particularly the girl with the straight blonde hair. A moment later, when a porter popped out of a cellar door with a pail and a mop, the girls suggested they get out of his way and take a table in the rear.

"Wait a second," said Suzy. "We have to get Eric another beer first." Eric couldn't believe his ears.

"Way to go," said Suzy as the newly formed foursome took their seats in a red leatherette booth. "That really woke everybody up. Bet you dropped it on purpose."

"No, no," Eric protested. But no one would believe him.

"Eric's like that," said Bud. "He looks quiet and innocent but just when you least expect it, he does something that really blows everybody's mind." The girls studied Eric with admiration, and he smiled over at Bud, thinking to himself, *Now that's what I call a friend.*

The rest of the evening was a ball. They drank and talked and laughed, and even though Eric kept on neurotically falling into states where he thought both girls were mad for his friend and only tolerating him, he survived. Later in the night when somebody at the other end of the bar let a beer bottle slip out of his grasp, Suzy said, "Ah, that guy's an amateur compared to you. His didn't make half as much noise." *God,* Eric thought, *here I am in torn pants with an unwashed, unshaved face having more fun with a woman than I've had in years.*

When the bar closed, the four young people headed out to Bud's car. Eric was wondering about the seating arrangements, but when he climbed in the back seat first, Suzy dove in after him. The girls suggested the boys come back to their apartment for coffee before the drive back to Jersey. Within moments Bud and the other girl disappeared into the rear room, leaving Suzy and Eric alone in the kitchen/dining/living room.

"Sit over here," said Suzy, patting the couch next to her. And very sweetly and gently and affectionately she put her arm around him and kissed him on the cheek. "I think you're really nice," she whispered. "I did the moment I saw you. You're friend is handsome, but not my type. You look more interesting, more sensitive. I like boys who look like that." Once again Eric was having difficulty believing that this incredibly pretty, interesting, vivacious girl was talking to him. And hugging him. And enjoying being with him. And to think, his friend Bud could barely get him out of the house that night!

Suzy and Eric went out together for the next several months and had a ball. He saw her dance at recitals at Julliard, and she came and watched him play touch football in Central Park. They stuffed themselves on Chinese food in Chinatown, on linguini and gnocchi in Little Italy. It was one of the pleasantest and most romantic relationships Eric ever had. We're not going to go into how Eric and Suzy finally grew apart. Breaking up is hardly the purpose of this book. Suffice it to say that it was fairly typical of the way most young adults drift out of a relationship. The important thing to focus on here is how the entire incident so powerfully affected his life. Eric learned something momentous, revelatory, apocalyptic that evening at the West End. And that is that you *don't* have to love yourself for other people to like you. You don't even have to like yourself. Some of the time you can downright hate yourself and still others may be attracted to you. Look at Eric on the night we've just described. He hated the way he looked that night, especially in comparison to his handsome friend. Nor was he very bullish about his personality, his wit, his charm. And yet somehow, some way, he wound up beginning a relationship with a lovely and exciting woman, someone whose love and affection he could only have *dreamed* he'd ever win.

So now, of course, whenever we read or hear that before anyone else can love you, you have to love yourself, our response is an immediate and forceful "Bull!" You can't *learn* to love yourself. Love is something you either feel or don't feel. If you don't feel it, no amount of willing or pep-talking or sermonizing is going to *make* you feel it. In fact, you'll probably just wind up driving yourself crazy in the process of trying.

No, learning to love yourself is *not* the key to getting over your shyness, not the one change you have to undergo to start meeting people with whom you can have a wonderful and loving relationship. Our experience has been that self-love is something yu're either born with, or something your parents instill in you at an early age, or something you gain through accomplishment and by meeting challenges. To sit around and try to talk yourself into it is merely a waste of time—and not nearly so important as most self-help books would have you believe.

The real key to conquering shyness is simply to learn how to stop acting shy. And in many ways this is every bit as simple and as basic as it sounds. Conquering shyness is not a mystical, spiritual process like learning how to be a great painter or poet. It's often lumped in that category of mystical "overcomings" . . . but the truth is, conquering shyness is a lot closer to learning how to hit a good backhand or build a garage or a barn. Now we've read most of the literature on shyness, and it's true that a lot of it would have you believe that the journey from shy to unshy is somehow undefinable, the result of deep psychological changes within your unconscious mind that are triggered by discovering how to think or feel a certain way. But we don't agree with that at all. We think you can learn how to act unshy in the same way you can learn how to stroke a golf ball or knit or tap dance, by practicing certain simple, basic, easy-to-understand techniques over and over again, not techniques like chanting a mantra or telling yourself you love yourself with as much enthusiasm and passion as you can manage. We think that's pure, unadulterated baloney guaranteed to continue to keep you in your room alone. No, the techniques for learning how to act unshy are as concrete and practical and "do-able" as hitting a tennis ball against a backboard for a half an hour every day.

Now you've probably noticed that we keep on writing "act" unshy rather than "be" unshy. We do it for a purpose. We're not sure you will ever be unshy. Once you're shy we're pretty certain you're going to retain your shyness for the rest of your life. But that's okay. In fact it's fine. Your shyness is an integral part of you, and is probably a key. ingredient in your charm, your creativity, your very essence. The major victory we're going to help you achieve is to *act* unshy because once you learn that, you will no longer suffer the consequences of living the shy life style.

You see, by learning to act unshy you begin automatically to start connecting with other people. You almost cannot fail. You, of course, may continue to feel as shaky and unconfident on the inside as you've always felt. But that doesn't matter. That's something only you will know for sure. The people you meet will see you as pleasant, relaxed, communicative, and outgoing. They don't have X-ray vision, and they'll have no inkling of the churning and turmoil that may be vibrating in your psyche. Thus, they'll respond to you positively, warmly, and affectionately. And once that happens the rest is easy.

Now perhaps you are thinking, *Gee, if all it takes is acting unshy, who needs this book? I know how to act unshy. It looks easy.*

Well, you're right about one thing. It is pretty easy to act unshy—once you know how. The problem is . . . MOST SHY PEOPLE HAVEN'T THE FAINTEST IDEA HOW TO ACT UNSHY.

Oh, they may think they do. And that it's just their shyness that is keeping them from acting that way. But the reality is they *don't* know how to act unshy. And it's that more than anything that is contributing to their isolation from the people they want to get close to.

This is why we are so passionate in our faith that this book can help you conquer your shyness. Because it shows you, step by basic step, exactly what it takes to appear unshy. There's no mystery to it, no magic, no luck. There's no fancy philosophizing—or at least very little of it—and no complicated psychological schema. For the most part you'll find just practical, tangible, eminently executable exercises and ideas that you can put into practice the very instant you open the book. Rather than present you with an obscure, mystical, amorphous program that you're never quite sure you're mastering, something that is purported to instill superconfidence via osmosis, our *Shy Person's Guide to Love and Loving* shows you in plain, simple language how to put one foot after another on your march to a happier, more fulfilling love life.

Some of the things we ask you to do are fun, some take a little bit of courage, but all of them are well within your capability and all of them will take you forward. And more importantly, all of them are concrete and precise and as achievable as digging a six-inch hole in your garden or mixing half a pot of peat moss with half a pot of top soil.

You know, to a greater or lesser degree, all of us are shy. All of us feel a battle being waged within us. On one hand we want to get out of ourselves and socialize with others. Still, another part of us wants to retreat to greater and more total absorption with self. It's literally like a tug-of-war—to get out of ourselves and at the same time to withdraw into our shell. Unfortunately, for some of us advance is difficult and retreat comfortable and easy. Some of us feel more acutely self-conscious the more we open ourselves up to the scrutiny of our peers. The goal of this book is to help those who find it difficult to advance to do it anyway. For it is this more than anything that will help the overly shy find the love and romance that makes life so much more livable. We've discovered that with a little bit of know-how it's easy to stop acting shy. And we're going to show you exactly how to go about it.

1

Incurable You

As YOU begin to read this book you are probably wrestling with an intense negative feeling: I am incurable. *Nothing will help my shyness.*

Don't worry. You are not alone. Almost anyone who has suffered the pain and loneliness of shyness has shared these emotions. In the privacy of a personal interview most shy people admit to a suffocating feeling of hopelessness and helplessness. They think of their shyness as bedrock, immoveable—the real them. No matter how many discotheques, office parties, mixers, and singles weekends they attend, they believe nothing will do any good.

And this notion has kept many shy people from taking any positive action to get over their shyness. "Ten years from now," says one young woman, a commercial banker, "I can picture myself married with a couple of kids and a nice house in the country. But to tell you the truth I haven't the faintest idea of how any of this will come about. Sometimes it seems so far away, like it'll never happen, like I'll never get any better. I go to parties and alumni dances and belong to my tenant's association and I take art classes at the local city college. But I never really feel anything is going to come of it. My shyness always seems to get in the way; nothing does any good."

Well, you know something? You aren't incurable; you couldn't be more curable. That is a fact, and by the time you've finished this book you'll know it's true.

There is a television cartoon about a man trying to dig his way out of a prison. He shoveled and shoveled, and when he still hadn't reached freedom, he gave up. Only the viewer could see that if he'd kept on digging a moment longer he would have broken through the thin crust separating him from the outside world.

In many cases shyness is nothing more than a thin crust, a brittle veneer that is keeping a potentially happy, social, engagé person cut off from the love and romance for which she or he yearns. Prod that crust a little, challenge it, keep on pecking away at it, and one day, often when you least expect, it'll break. And when it does the transformation from lonely and inward to outgoing and social can be astonishingly swift.

Many psychiatrists and psychologists agree. Dr. Sam Perry of Cornell University Medical Center and Dr. Bob Glick of Columbia Presbyterian Medical Center report that shyness is one of the easiest problems to treat. They have had their shy patients out and about, going to parties, going on dates, and having fun after just a few sessions. The results are remarkable. Shyness is eminently curable compared to other common problems, such as stuttering or depression.

Dr. Philip Zimbardo, a well-known shyness expert on the West Coast, runs a shyness clinic where he's been able to take shy people and teach them social self-confidence with great effectiveness. He shows them how to be more outgoing, less inward, and within weeks many of them find that their social and love lives have improved dramatically.

Ronald, a college student, was a brilliant physicist but almost a recluse, so great was his fear of social situations. He would stand stiffly in the corner at mixers and student-faculty parties, and always looked to be in tremendous discomfort, if not downright pain. It seemed that he would have given anything to get back to his room and his beloved physics books. He once mournfully admitted that he didn't know why he went to these functions since he had never met anyone before and couldn't imagine doing so in the future.

Then, toward the end of his senior year, Ronald underwent an enormous change. At a spring dance at the student union, Patti, a bright pretty girl from one of his courses, came up to him and asked if she could borrow his notes, explaining she had missed four lectures in a row and she knew that if anybody had taken good notes it'd been Ronald. When she mentioned how anxious she was about the upcoming mid-semester exam, Ronald somehow managed to sputter out an offer of help. Patti leapt at the suggestion, and every night for the next week Ronald and Patti spent hours going over Ronald's notes together. But that wasn't all that was happening. Slowly but surely Patti was beginning to develop quite a crush on Ronald. On the day they got their exams back (Patti got a B+, her highest physics grade ever) she asked Ronald to a party at her sorority house. Clinging to his arm, laying her head affectionately on his shoulder, she introduced Ronald all around to her friends as the genius who had helped her pass physics. Patti's absolute ease with other people began to sweep over Ronald. With Patti at his side, he no longer seemed as frightened by others as he did when on his own.

The important thing to note is that Ronald, who had attended college functions with a suffocating sense of pessimism and failure, suddenly found himself totally and gloriously relieved of his aloneness, his sense of separation. It happened when he was expecting it least, when he was most certain that nothing would do any good.

One day Ronald was feeling thoroughly incurable. The next day he was happily in love. And this isn't by any means an isolated phenomenon. It happens all the time. And it can happen to you no matter how incurable you feel.

Don't let your sense of incurableness keep you from pursuing the techniques in this book. You'll be asked to go to dances at which you're sure you'll meet no one, to talk with people you're not interested in or who you're convinced are not interested in you. This will often feel useless, futile, as if it's not doing any good. But you should do it anyway. One day soon, a month from now, two Monday's hence, and maybe even tomorrow, incurable old you will find yourself enjoying an exciting, comfortable, loving relationship.

2

Opening Up About Your Shyness

ONE OF the traits that keeps shy people shy is that they are often unable to talk about their shyness. It embarrasses them. To the shy person, shyness is not unlike a disfiguring affliction, something you just don't discuss. A chubby person will query a friend about a particular diet. Someone who is having trouble with her eyesight might ask an acquaintance to recommend a good optometrist. Heavy smokers are often heard to complain aloud about their inability to give up cigarettes. But rarely do shy people ever mention how unhappy they are with their shyness.

And of course this just helps keep the whole business of shyness that much more secretive and undercover. Which in turn makes shyness that much harder to cure. The problem keeps on getting worse and worse, and yet the sufferer stoically refuses to seek help. Imagine what would happen if you had a bad toothache, and instead of going to a dentist you did nothing and simply endured it. Living alone with your shyness can be just as destructive to your health. You may not feel as intensely in pain as you do with a decaying tooth, but that's because the pain is something that started out years ago on a fairly low level and you've become used to it. What makes it so much more dangerous than a bad toothache is that you don't even *feel* it getting worse. Yet it does. The longer you keep your shyness under wraps, the longer you go without sharing it with your friends or parents or the people who love you, the harder it becomes to do so. You grow more set in your ways, more internal, more rigidly on guard. This is not meant to frighten you but to motivate you. The sooner you can bring yourself to begin to talk about your shyness with others, to explore it openly, to see that it is *not* a hideous social stigma to be ashamed of, but rather a very common problem shared by millions, the easier it is to be cured of it.

The recommendation in this chapter is simply this: Talk about your shyness. With a good friend, with a parent, with a dear sibling, or with anyone with whom you feel comfortable and safe. It doesn't really matter who the person is, as long as you begin talking.

That very act—talking about your shyness—will help you to overcome it. No one is quite sure of the internal psychodynamics that come into play when a shy person opens up to another about his or her shyness. But somehow it eases the misery one feels about the problem and makes one feel less alone and less isolated. And once that occurs, the cure process has begun. The road to a more active, participatory social life has been embarked upon and other, more advanced steps can be taken. For some persons the act of talking about their shyness is the very first step to getting better.

First of all, there's the problem of finding the right person to talk to. And then after that there's the terrifying chore of actually getting the words out. You will be uncomfortable and may even feel this is an impossible task. The fact is, though, that once you can bring yourself to begin talking, the words soon just pour out.

It becomes easy and pleasant and feels, oh, so comforting and helpful. Another pleasant discovery you'll make is that the person you're talking to will respond not in the alarmed, standoffish manner you're anticipating, but warmly and sympathetically. It happens nearly everytime.

HOW TO FIND SOMEONE WITH WHOM TO DISCUSS YOUR SHYNESS

For some of you this will be easy. Sure, you're shy, but you do have a few close friends. Or a brother or a sister to whom you can open your heart. And many of you, of course, have a mother or a father or even both who would welcome the opportunity to help. But unfortunately there are others who are so shy you don't have anyone you feel close to. For you, here's some advice: See if you can think of anyone in your professional life who might make a good confidant. If you are at school, a guidance counselor or kindly teacher might be a good choice. If you work, perhaps someone in your personnel department would be good to talk to. Or maybe your company even has a staff psychologist for its employees. Failing that, what about your clergyman or physician? If you still don't feel comfortable with any of these people, then we suggest you seek out the name of a good therapist or counselor. For those of you who still think therapy is only for mentally or emotionally disturbed people, you'd better change your thinking. Statistics show that one out of every two people in America has received personal therapy or counseling of some kind at some time in their lives. So seeking therapy is not something you should view as carrying a social stigma. It is almost as natural today as going to the dentist for a toothache.

How do you go about finding a good therapist? It's easy. Call up your local hospital or state board of health to recommend a qualified practitioner. Or call your local Department of Mental Health. There is no need to feel frightened or nervous—these places are staffed by friendly, understanding, and highly qualified personnel. No one will laugh at you or scorn you. These agencies exist for the sole purpose of helping you.

You can explain that you want to speak to a therapist about your shyness problem, and the agency will simply set up an appointment with a certified counselor. In most states and counties you will be charged according to your ability to pay, but under no circumstances will it be more than fifteen dollars.

The point of this little exercise is to show you how easy it is to get qualified professional help if there's no one else around you feel comfortable talking to. And if you don't want to call the health clinic yourself, maybe a friend or relative will do it for you. This isn't a recommendation, of course, that you enter therapy on a long-term basis.

You may feel you have serious problems but your basic need is nothing more than to conquer your shyness and start meeting and dating new people. If you can't get up the courage to talk to someone with whom you are personally acquainted, a session or two with a qualified and sympathetic therapist can be a great help in starting to dismantle your shyness problem.

HOW TO START TALKING ABOUT YOUR SHYNESS

Again, to some this is going to sound excessively fundamental. You just open your mouth and start talking. Well, if this is how you feel about it, fine. Begin. This is a sign that you may be a lot less shy than you think. But for those of you to whom this sounds like an impossible task, one fraught with peril and embarrassment, follow these instructions. Casually mention to the confidant you've selected that you'd like to discuss something with him at his convenience. What would be a good time? A good place? Hopefully he will suggest a quiet, private area. If not, suggest one yourself, explaining the matter you want to discuss is somewhat confidential. There is nothing wrong, of course, in just dropping in on a parent or friend or fellow office worker without setting up an appointment. But if you do and then are unable to bring up your shyness, set up a formal apointment for the future. This will put a little more pressure on you to open up. (After all, you'd feel a bit silly after arousing his curiosity with a request for a private audience if you babble on about his great new desk.)

People are almost without exception helpful and comforting when you come to them for advice about your shyness. In fact you'll probably be astonished at what lengths they will go to to help you meet and get to know others.

During an awful, lonely weekend at the Jersey shore many years ago, Rodger confided to a friend that he was just too afraid of rejection to approach any girls at the myriad singles bars he and pals were touring. The friend put his arm around Rodger, marched him over to the first attractive girl they came to, and said, "Miss, I'd like you to meet my friend Rodger, one of the greatest lovers in all of Ocean City, if not the entire East Coast." Everybody laughed, and within minutes Rodger and the girl were chatting like old friends.

The point of this chapter, however, is not *what* the people you talk to about your shyness will offer you in the way of help, but that you simply open up about your shyness. That is the key to getting better, the very act of opening up. Anything else that results is gravy. But if all that you accomplish is that you talk— even if your listener seems a trifle cold or disinterested—you should still consider yourself triumphant. You have brought your shyness out of the closet and that is what counts on the road to getting better.

3

Shyness Roots

WHEN JOANN was in the fifth grade, she was bright and sensitive, but already five feet eight inches in height. She was the tallest kid in her class, boys included, and she used to take quite a ribbing for it. Perhaps a less sensitive child would have ignored the barbs and taunts, but JoAnn seemed incapable of the kind of tough "sticks-and-stones-will-break-my-bones" attitude that the not-so-shy are invariably born with and the very shy long for.

Anyway, JoAnn drew further and further into herself as her grammar school years came to an end, and during high school she seemed to disappear altogether. By this time, of course, many of the other kids had caught up with JoAnn in height, and she no longer stood out so blatantly. But apparently that didn't help to relieve her shyness. If anyone noticed or talked about her at all, it was only to remark about what a "brain" she was. Whenever the class was stumped by a particularly tough

24

question, the teacher would call upon a reluctant JoAnn who, turning crimson, would answer it flawlessly. Those who knew her from back in grade school attributed her embarrassment to her "tall days" in the fifth grade. Feeling "different" was something that had become ingrained when she was ten years old; even though she was no longer unusually tall, there was no escaping the memory of it.

For the longest time JoAnn made the same assumption about herself. Just as the formerly obese are never really able to think of themselves as thin, even when they've dieted or exercised themselves down to a nice normal waistline, JoAnn thought of herself as a tall person, a freak, someone with a physical deformity that just couldn't be disguised. Or at least that's what she told herself.

I'll never feel comfortable around other people because I've had such a traumatic childhood. Even if I'm no longer a funny-looking, tall person on the outside, I'm a tall person on the inside and I'll never get over it if I live a million years. None of this ever really rang quite true in her mind or in her heart, but it *seemed* a logical explanation for her shyness. And so for years JoAnn never questioned it.

When JoAnn was a sophomore in college, her family moved to a town seven miles from the community where she grew up. Her father had been doing very well in business and decided he wanted to live in a grander house in a more fashionable neighborhood. JoAnn's mother was less than enthusiastic about the move because she was president of her local Woman's Club, a member of the board of the PTA, and one of the most popular, respected women in town. She had dozens of friends, and when she drove down to the post office or the grocery store, she was greeted by just about everyone.

In the town to which they moved, JoAnn's parents hardly knew anyone. To help them meet new people they joined a country club less than a mile from their house and spent the summer cultivating friendships around the pool and on the golf course. JoAnn hated the place, found it phony and overdone and crass. Instead, she stayed in her room, reading, writing, and dreaming about boys. She couldn't wait until college was back in session so that maybe, just maybe, she would meet someone in one of her classes. She certainly wasn't going to meet a man at home.

One particularly hot August day JoAnn let her mother talk her into coming to the pool at the club. The cabana boy arranged mattresses for them, and then the two women, mother and daughter, lay back in the sun. An hour went by. And then another. JoAnn kept on looking up from her book at her mother. Something was wrong. She couldn't put her finger on it. Every time someone walked by, her mother would look at the person and begin humming nervously to herself. Finally, a little after lunch, two self-assured-looking women in ultrafashionable bathing suits plopped themselves down near JoAnn and her mother. A minute later JoAnn's mother began humming again, staring at the two women like a bird dog. But every time they looked over she averted her eyes. And all the while she kept on humming to herself.

"Oh, hello, Liz," one of the women said after finally catching JoAnn's mother staring at her.

"Hi," her mother answered. Then quietly to JoAnn, "Come on over, dear. I want you to meet some very nice people."

JoAnn shrugged and stood up, and then she and her mother walked over to the two women in the stylish bathing suits, all the while JoAnn's mother humming under her breath to beat the band. For the life of her, JoAnn couldn't understand what her mother was so tense about. Asking a good-looking boy in your zoology class if you could borrow his notes was one thing, but saying hello to two people of the same sex . . . why even JoAnn wasn't so shy that she was made uncomfortable by it. She'd never seen her mother looking so nervous before. Or had she? For the first time in her life JoAnn actually found herself feeling more competent, more grown-up than this woman who had always seemed like such a self-contained dynamo to her.

Over the next few weeks JoAnn accompanied her mother to

the club several more times, and on each occasion when they chatted with people around the pool, JoAnn could hear her mother humming nervously under her breath. She wondered if her mother was aware of what she was doing. And it made her realize that this social, comfortable, breezy, mother of hers was, underneath it all, just as shy and insecure as she was. And that's when it occurred to JoAnn that perhaps it wasn't her premature tallness at all that had made her feel so shy.

After all, she'd always been secretly proud of her height. It had given her a sense of superiority, power, made her feel older and more grown-up than the other kids. When they'd taunted her about it, she had often thought they were just jealous.

No, perhaps the real reason she acted so damn shy was that she'd picked it up from her mother. Now *this* rang a chord much truer and more emotional. She'd been hearing her mother hum nervously under her breath since babyhood, every time the woman felt uncomfortable or faced with possible rejection. No wonder JoAnn had always felt so ill-at-ease when meeting new people. She'd learned it from her role model, from the person she'd been closer to than anyone else in the world.

The very act of discovering the roots of her shyness was immensely liberating. For one thing, JoAnn felt far less intimidated by her mother. For years she'd been awed, over-whelmed by her mother's seemingly fearless approach to mixing with others. To discover that her mother was perhaps even shyer than she made her feel less alone, less a family "freak." Why, in certain ways it made her feel just the slightest bit superior to her mother.

Before long JoAnn was feeling less self-conscious and more socially aggressive. She was still tall and still remarkably bright, but in most other respects she seemed dramatically different. After college JoAnn was able to get a good job working in the publishing field. She was part of a big circle of friends, mostly young would-be novelists who were interested in writing, if not the Great American Novel, at least one that would make them rich. She lived with an imposing-looking man in his forties, a reasonably well-known playright who was in the process of getting out of a long and loveless marriage in the suburbs. JoAnn seemed as at ease now as any of the other bright, self-assured people around her office. What a contrast from the crimson-faced shrinking violet she was back in grade school.

Today, JoAnn often tells the story of her humming mother. "Ever since then," she explains, "I stopped being so uptight about my shyness. It just didn't seem such a stigma anymore. I figured if this wonderful woman who everybody in town loved and respected was shy, then I could be shy, too, and not feel like such a weirdo. Maybe realizing that my mother was shy, yet had still managed to find herself a husband and a lot of friends, gave me hope. Who knows? All I know for sure is that it helped."

By discovering where your shyness came from, it sometimes loses a little of its sting, its ability to paralyze you. So see if you can figure out exactly what it is that has left you so vulnerable to your shyness. Free associate. Let your mind drift. Think of your mother and your father. How do they behave when meeting new people? At parties? Business functions? Picture their faces when shaking hands with important clients or people they'd like to impress. Chances are you'll discover your shyness is a learned response picked up from one of your parents, perhaps even both of them. And once you realize that, you may very well feel that shyness isn't the hideous stigma you thought it was, that it's just a trait that's been in the family all along.

This is not to say, of course, that this simple realization will send you bolting out of the house to introduce yourself to the next gorgeous stranger that happens by. But isolating shyness' roots has helped to unloosen the vise in which shyness holds so many good people a prisoner.

4

Hidden Payoff

THIS IS going to sound very blunt—it's not to be unkind but to help you uncover a possible truth about yourself that you may never have realized: YOU LIKE BEING ṢHY!

You probably think you hate being shy, you can't stand it, and you insist you want to be unshy, but the actuality is . . . you may like being shy. Why? Because your shyness is, by now, totally, thoroughly comfortable.

While you may not be aware of it, this is a notion that psychiatrists often refer to as the "hidden payoff" of shyness. Shyness, you see, gives a person an excuse for staying home at night, for not going to parties, and for avoiding singles bars. As long as you're shy, you can be an "unsocial" being and you never take the risk of exposing yourself to others.

Take any night in recent memory when you even half-wanted to go out. Perhaps you thought you'd try the new disco around the corner, or maybe a friend told you about a party in town. But instead of going out you gave in to inertia, or to an impulse to take it easy, and ended up staying home. You turned on the television, curled up in your favorite corner of the couch, got into comfortable clothes, and made yourself a light snack. Maybe you were a little disappointed that you had lost the battle to go out and that you were alone doing nothing. But on the other hand, it was very comfortable to be hanging out with yourself . . . too comfortable. There you were all alone, on a date with yourself, contemplating yourself, thinking about yourself, and bathing in your narcisssism. You liked it . . . it was easy, it was unchallenging. If you didn't like it, wouldn't you have gone out hours ago?

By remaining shy you can avoid taking social risks and possibly exposing yourself to failure. Or maybe even more frightening, *success*. Shyness protects you from situations that you fear may cause you humilation or discomfort. You are so preoccupied with yourself that anyone, anything, any occasion that might take you out of yourself is to be avoided. *That* is the secret truth of shyness. That's why shy people so often feel panicky when meeting a new person . . . not only because they're afraid of being rejected, which hurts, but also because they're afraid they'll be accepted, which will in turn break up the romance with themselves and force them to talk to, or laugh with, or take an interest in, someone else.

Think about it. Your situation will never change by contemplating various theories about your shyness. It changes only when you take action to get out. If your choice is to remain curled up on your couch with a book or to watch television, weekend after weekend, year after year, no matter how long you contemplate your shyness your social situation won't improve. And the longer you postpone changing your habits, the harder it will be to do so. These habits can get *very* comfortable.

Where does it say you have to be comfortable all the time? No human or animal is. Part of life and part of being a healthy human being is learning how to weather the uncomfortable times. They pass—and you emerge from the storm stronger, somehow cleansed, and you like yourself better. You can grow into a socially active person. You can't do it by staying in and being comfortable. You can do it by challenging yourself, going out, being a little uncomfortable at first, but eventually outgrowing that discomfort.

Think of the last time you had a difficult assignment in school or at work. While you were completing it, the hard work and tension all but drove you up the wall. But now you only remember the satisfaction of a job well done. The memory of all that work has practically disappeared. And you'll have the same experience when you finally take positive action to overcome your shyness. There will be discomfort, maybe even some embarrassment or pain. But in a few months you won't remember what it was like to feel painfully shy. With social growth there is pain, but it's worth it if in the end you discover the beauty of being with others.

The comfort or enjoyment you feel staying home simply isn't true comfort. Don't kid yourself. Any brief discomfort you may feel while you are learning to act unshy breeds true comfort later on. And the enjoyment of a delicious, exciting, intimate love life is a thousand times more enjoyable than being home and safe and *alone*.

5

Shyness Is Not a Neon Sign

WHEN YOU walk into a party, you probably feel your shyness is standing out like a day-glo shirt in a dark disco or a huge pimple on your nose, and it is so loud people can hear it. But do you know something? No one can tell you're shy right off the bat. The truth is, unless you're as striking as a movie star, singing loudly to yourself, or wearing a vampire costume, no one's even noticing you. The rest of the people at the party are all too busy worrying about themselves to be concerned about you.

Many shy friends, however, report that whenever they step into a party they get the feeling that everyone in the room turns to look at them. And not only do they look, they laugh. And sneer. And pass judgment.

"How can we ever hope to meet anyone," shy people ask, "when we're spotted as losers the instant we enter a room?

Shyness is written all over our faces. No one'll want to ever talk to us, much less dance, flirt, neck, or leave with us."

Our response to this plaintive tale of woe, shy people, is that you are *not* marked as a loser the instant you enter a party. More than likely, you're hardly noticed. The physical manifestations of shyness—blushing, slouching, averted eyes—none of these is readily visible to the casual observer. So there is no reason in the world for shy persons to feel the game is lost before they even begin to play.

The reason it's so important for you to understand this is that it can help you develop a whole new attitude toward party-going. Instead of panicking the moment you arrive at an affair, maybe from now on you'll realize that you're virtually invisible and can take all the time in the world to get your courage up.

You don't have to rush into frenzied mixing to prove to others you're every bit as social as they are. Remember, they're not even aware you are there yet. So slow down and get your bearings. Visit the john and check your hair. Have a drink to calm you down if you feel like it. Observe the other guests. See them as mannequins in a store window. Keep feeling invisible and relaxed.

Then begin to circulate. Do it easily, casually. Just walk around until you feel yourself falling naturally into a group situation or until you can use some of your small-talk skill. And if nothing happens, and you're just standing there alone for a few minutes, that's okay too. No one is watching you but yourself.

The other guests are all wondering not whether you mingle well, but whether they should have worn a different dress, if they should cross their legs on a crowded couch, or if the foot deodorant in their shoes is holding up.

Your shyness is not a blotch. Not a rash. Not a neon sign. It is invisible.

When you're ready to take another pass through the crowd, go right ahead. But go at your own chosen speed. Remember, no one knows you're there until you approach them. Your slate is clean. There are no negative marks against you. Only you know you're shy. And armed with the antishyness techniques in this book, you will learn how to disguise that fact. Which is why when you do finally make up your mind to say hello, the person you speak to is going to respond warmly, happily, and pleasantly.

6

The Tyranny of Shyness:
How to Overthrow It

HAS ANYTHING like this ever happened to you? You are in your office and someone comes buzzing by saying, "Hey, there's a surprise party in the Conference Room at five o'clock. Wine and cheese and good music. We're celebrating Mike's promotion. Want to come?"

"Sure," you say. "Why not?" Then you add, "That is, if I can break free from all this work." (That's your insurance policy.) During the course of the afternoon, the party keeps popping into your mind. Maybe now you can finally meet some of the people who were only passing acquaintances around the office. Wine and cheese sounds like fun. And you have nowhere to go after work.

But an hour or two later, without quite realizing how it's snuck up on you, the tyranny of shyness has you in its grip. Like an angel (or devil) of doubt, it seats itself on the throne in your mind and issues orders: "How can you go? Look at all that work you have to do. You'll have to stay late. Or, if you rush you'll do it all wrong. Besides, you promised to call your mother long distance, and you can't make that phone call from your desk. No doubt the cheese will be left over from the last office party, and they probably added water to the wine. Anyway, who cares about Mike, it was time you got promoted. And the people who always turn out for these things, what bores. They're either close to retirement, dull, or only hanging around because they have nothing better to do with their time. Go to an office party? Why waste your time?"

What's really happening here? The tyranny of shyness is taking over, and under its spell you really do think you have to call home, that the food will be awful, and that the people will be uninteresting. So, you don't go. Not because of any undeniable truth to the reasons you've invented, but because of your shyness. It's not your fear that you won't like the party that's making you so reluctant to go, but that the party (and the people there) won't like you. Most people are shy in some situations. But they *can act unshy* and wouldn't think twice about going to an office party. They'd stop in and if it suited them they'd stay. If not, they would have some wine, congratulate Mike, socialize a little, and split. No big deal.

But it is hard to break away from the tyranny of shyness. And toward this end you'll be shown a list of some of the shy person's classic excuses in a situation like the one described above. Don't be surprised if they seem familiar. What these doubts really say is "Now, wait a second, you're not going anywhere." But we feel that any social event, no matter how ordinary or boring it might seem, is a good opportunity for you to get out of yourself. By listing these tyrannic doubts you'll have a chance to recognize them. Once you spot them you'll be better equipped to ward them off before they ruin a good evening. Read the list over and see if a few of your favorites aren't included:

- I feel sick. I'm coming down with something.
- I haven't got anything to wear.
- You can't meet anyone in a place like that.
- I don't know how to get there.
- How will I get home?
- Five dollars! That's too much to pay to get in. I'm not a sucker.
- None of my friends will go with me.
- I'm ten pounds overweight. I don't look right.
- Next week, maybe, when I get my contact lenses.
- Any other night but tonight. My favorite program's on television.
- What? And miss the football game?
- I simply cannot put this book down.
- It's too cold out. I'll get the flu.
- It's too hot out. I'll sweat.
- Too much crime on the streets. If they had the dance at three in the afternoon, I might consider it.
- I can't dance.
- I'm no good at outdoor sports.
- I never understand lectures.
- You can't meet anyone in art museums anymore. They did that in the fifties.
- Hayride? I have hay fever.
- Go swimming? I'm afraid of the water.
- The people aren't cultured. No one of my taste will be there.
- That's a "lonelyhearts" thing. Forget it.

Perhaps you can identify with a few of the above. (There are probably hundreds more that you could add.) All shy people have been guilty of using these excuses more than a few times when looking for a reason *not* to go out. So the next time you have somewhere to go and a doubt or excuse creeps into your mind, ask yourself this: Is that the real reason I'm not going, or has the tyranny of shyness begun to take effect?

If you really want to get over your shyness, stand up to your doubts. Anytime you can conquer a doubt before it does you in and leaves you out, you win a battle against the tyranny of shyness. And soon you'll win the war.

7

Fantasy World:
Stop, You Want to Get Off

YOU ALL know what fantasies are. Those rich, perfect daydreams you spin that are better than any Hollywood film. More satisfying is the fact that you produce, direct, and star in each of these luscious, made-to-order, happy-ending confections.

Many self-help books encourage exploring your dreams and fantasies, analyzing them, and looking for clues in them, but perhaps they're not worth spending all that much time with. To an extent fantasizing does release the imagination, can give your repressed mind an airing, and can even motivate you into positive action.

But the problem is shy people spend an inordinate amount of time engaged in fantasizing. They fantasize about being smart, pretty, sexy, exciting, daring, and provocative. They spend hours daydreaming about being the life of the party, about a perfect date with Cheryl Tiegs or Jon Voight, about the closeness of a romantic relationship, and about passionate lovemaking with an attractive mate. Their fantasies become so complex, so vivid, and so gratifying in a perverse sort of way, that colorful fantasizing literally replaces the pursuit of pleasurable things in the real world.

Instead of challenging him or herself to actually find an attractive date, or to discover the excitement of a real and close relationship, the shy person immerses him or herself in the depths of fantasy. It's so much easier and so much less chancy. This, of course, leads to a self-defeating cycle. Real life is boring, fantasy life is satisfying. So the shy person devotes more and more time to fantasizing, finally spending an unreasonable amount of time at it. And that's unhealthy.

The next question is, what is reasonable? Forty-five minutes a day is the maximum amount of time that should be spent in fantasy. Any more than that will begin to interfere with the pursuit of a full, active, and real social life.

Unfortunately, it is safer, easier, and more comfortable for the shy person to escape into fantasy than to face the difficulties of becoming active socially. But when your whole life consists of rich, wild, unrealistic fantasy, vitually nothing in the real world will seem satisfying. For example, take the young adolescent boys and girls who have heard for years about the pleasures of sex. They imagine that the first time they have intercourse they will see stars, their hearts will pound, and they will have frantic, multiple orgasms. Unfortunately first sexual experiences rarely meet these expectations, and they are naturally disappointed. Not until they abandon their sexual fantasies and begin to enjoy the closeness of another real human being do they find the true beauty and pleasures of sex.

Shy people often have favorite fantasies. Cindi's was a full-scale wedding fantasy that obsessed her for years. It was complete with six bridesmaids dressed in Cindi's favorite shade of blue, and every good-looking man she met was inserted into the role of groom. This fantasy became so real to Cindi that she actually would walk into print shops to select a decorative wedding invitation design.

William relished the image of himself in a black leather jacket, leaning against his motorcycle, a cigarette dangling from his mouth as he played his favorite fantasy—Devastating Dude. He loved this fantasy because the prettiest girls always approached him and threw themselves all over him.

In fact, William admits he would climb into bed an hour or two early so he could pursue this fantasy to its fullest. Now, as a successful writer and businessman who has learned to act unshy, William no longer finds fantasizing as satisfying. Sometimes, on nights when he is having trouble falling asleep, he says he would welcome a fantasy but can no longer seem to dredge one up that's as much fun or as satisfying as his real life.

You're no doubt wondering how a person simply shuts down his mind during a full-blown fantasy. It is not easy, especially if you've fantasized heavily for years. But you can try a two-step method that will help tremendously if applied conscientiously.

The first step involves simply observing that you're fantasizing. Shy people can get so caught up in the creation of a fantasy that they actually tune themselves out from the real world. It is crucial therefore that you learn to recognize those times when you drift away in fantasy. This alone will help you see the unreality and wastefulness of it.

Second, you can use a technique called "thought stoppage." Thought stoppage involves recognizing the fantasy (step one) and then commanding the mind to stop thinking it. When you realize you are fantasizing you simply say out loud "STOP."

You'll find, at first, that rather than stopping the fantasy, this makes it more alluring. At that moment you must say "STOP" again. If you're in a crowded room and cannot blurt it out, then say "STOP" loudly in your mind. Continue to do this until the fantasy disappears. Better yet, seek out another activity. Find someone nearby to talk to. Bounce a ball. File your nails. You'll probably find yourself saying "STOP" a hundred times a day for a week. But in as short a time as two weeks you will have cut your fantasizing down to near zero.

Some people have fantasies which are so strong they carry a stick pin with them. When they say "STOP," they simultaneously poke themselves gently with the pin. Psychologists call this classic behavioral modification, specifically, operant conditioning, and it is very effective for changing unwanted behavior.

Louis was a librarian who helped locate research material for this book. He was thin, frail, timid-looking, and closely fit the stereotyped librarian image. He had practically no active social life, but he spent long hours engaged in elaborate fantasies.

In Louis's favorite and most frequent fantasy he would be studying Tolstoi's *War and Peace* in an isolated book rack when a gorgeous, curvaceous blonde would approach him. Looking longingly at him, she would whisper, "You must have a great mind. I think that's so sexy." She would stroke his hair and perform an erotic striptease while begging him to make love to her. He would smile and then wildly have intercourse with her there on the library floor.

Louis realized that his fantasies interfered with a real social life, but he complained that he couldn't help it. He would be sitting at his desk, and before he knew it he was far away in fantasy land.

Louis was counseled in the use of thought stoppage. He reported that the first day he used thought stoppage 347 times. The next day it was even more, 407 times. But each day after that he used it less and less. By the eleventh day Louis reported that he had brief fantasies only once or twice a day.

Learning to control fantasies is important for the shy person who wants to have a better social life, but it should be accompanied by a conscientious program to meet and date people. You can develop this by following the exercises set up in this book. In that way the enjoyment of a real and exciting social life replaces the need for an active fantasy life.

8

Unreasonable, Idealized Expectations

SILVIO IS an intelligent twenty-six-year-old junior accountant in a small firm. He is especially interesting because, unlike most shy people, Silvio expressed genuine anger over his shyness.

Silvio was making an encouraging and very admirable effort to disentangle himself from his shy habits. As hard as it was for him, he was attending more social functions and was even starting to make a few phone calls to female friends. Yet he continued to feel frustrated over his inability to meet more women.

One day, after he had just returned from lunch at a posh French restaurant, he looked angry and frustrated and was ranting that he'd never get over "this damn shyness!" He explained that he'd spotted the most fantastic-looking girl he had ever seen in his whole life seated on the other side of the restaurant. She had long, straight blonde hair, big liquid eyes,

43

and a figure so perfect every man in the room was staring at her, including, quite naturally, her luncheon companion, a dapper-looking chap in a pin-striped suit.

There Silvio sat, eating lunch, gazing at the blonde woman, unable to move. As he recounted the story he looked furious with himself. "Can you imagine," he complained, "letting the love of my life slip away from me like that. I finished my lunch, got up, walked out, and never even went up to her to ask her for her telephone number."

When Silvio finished his story, he looked downright guilty, almost enraged, as if he half-expected to be chastized for his shyness. No one, not even the most adventurous Casanova, would have had the nerve to approach a strange woman, no matter how attractive, when she was obviously having lunch with another man. For one thing, that man may well have been her husband. But even if he were only a boyfriend or a business associate, it would have been in bad taste to approach her.

When this was explained to Silvio, it eased his mind instantly. He admitted that once he had decided to become a "social person," he had begun to put great pressure on himself to meet and date people. He said that at parties he felt as if he were expected to speak with everyone. Instead of feeling sociable, friendly, and comfortable, he felt awkward, unnatural, and a little embarrassed.

The discomfort Silvio was feeling was due to unreasonable, idealized expectations of himself. It is not uncommon for shy people to suffer from this. They feel that if they go to a party they have to be charming, witty, and happy at all times. If they're at a singles bar or discotheque they feel they're failing unless they approach the most glamorous, glittery love objects in the room. Because their expectations are unreasonably high, they cannot help but fall short of them. The result is that shy people often feel crushed under a burden of unrelenting self-flagellation.

There are very few healthy people who don't feel sad at times or quiet or a little serious, and when they feel that way it effects them socially. The shy person should know that variations in moods are normal, and that no human being can expect to have a date every night or make a new friend every day. This would be an unreasonable request to make of the most unshy of people.

Try this little exercise. Think about the way you would expect a same-sex friend to act at a party. How should he (or she) look? Should he be dressed meticulously and formally, or casually and comfortably? How should he act? Should he be constantly laughing, smiling, telling jokes, and vying to be the center of attention? Or should he converse politely, tell a joke occasionally, but not be so talkative as to be overbearing? Include other characteristics typical of people in a social setting.

After you have completed your list, take a look at it. No doubt, the behavior you have outlined is not wild, outrageous, or extreme, but reasonable, normal behavior. Unfortunately, if you had done the same exercises listing expectations for yourself, you might have found them far more demanding than what anyone could expect from a normal human being.

Remember: DON'T EXPECT ANYMORE FROM YOUR-SELF THAN YOU WOULD REASONABLY EXPECT FROM ANOTHER HUMAN BEING.

While you are practicing the techniques in this book, try to keep your social goals within reach. Once you start to make unreasonable demands upon yourself, you increase the pressure and invite failure or setbacks. For now, establish smaller social goals and work your way up to your more fantastic ideas of social success. And those successes *will* come, if you follow these suggestions carefully.

In the next few weeks remember not to expect highly idealized, unreasonable things from yourself that even Warren Beatty or Diane Keaton couldn't achieve. You've been shy for a long time. Just give this book two months and be a little easier on yourself, and you'll soon be acting unshy and achieving social feats that Beatty and Keaton would be proud of!

9

Stop Dressing Shy

TAKE A minute to do something before you read this chapter. Go to your closet and look at your clothes, objectively. Look for color, style, and trendiness in fashion. Then come back and read this chapter.

While studying and analyzing and talking to shy people, one thing becomes apparent: They all tend to dress alike. Though their clothes are usually neat and clean and crisp, they are without fail conservative. There are no shocking pinks or glorious yellows. Hair styles on men and women are always carefully understated, never dramatic. Shy people dress *shy*. There's no flair, no pazazz, no sense of adventure in the way they express themselves through their clothes.

Some shy people realize this but rationalize it by saying they don't want to look tacky. It just wouldn't be them. They don't like trendy clothes because fashion is so fickle and unsensible.

But the fact remains that shy people seem to make an extra effort to dress in a way that *won't cause them to be noticed.*

Explore for a moment the folly of this. You go to an affair with other people in the hope of meeting someone with whom you can start a relationship. But if everything you do, the way you act, and even the clothes you wear, blend inconspicuously into the surroundings, how can you expect to meet anyone?

Shy people can and must entertain the notion of dressing with a little more flair. Think of it merely as packaging: your hair, your clothes, your jewelry. When you go shopping don't you automatically head for the brightest, shiniest, most appealing apple on the fruitstand? Well, with people it's very much the same. If you dress in a brighter, more exciting way, people will notice *and* be attracted to you.

You shouldn't get overly hung up on your appearance (you're undoubtedly too self-conscious as it is), but you should realize that the way you present yourself can serve you well in improving your social life. You're not advised to dress up in the latest garb of a Punk Rock star. You'd probably wind up feeling more shy than you do already. But you will notice positive results when you dress with more dash.

Eleanor was a very shy girl who moved to a southern city after graduation from a well-known woman's college. Four years at school had left her somewhat unconcerned about her clothes and when she started her new job as a legal aide her wardrobe was lacklustre.

Eleanor's new roommate in the city was a fashion conscious newspaper reporter with a varied and imaginative wardrobe. One evening Eleanor was removing some of her roommate's clothes from the couch when a chic, red satin blouse caught her eye. Having never owned anything like it, her temptation to try it on was overwhelming and she nervously slipped it on. What Eleanor saw almost made her gasp. The young woman with the slender waist staring back at her from the mirror looked like someone out of *Cosmopolitan.*

With encouragement from her roommate, Eleanor wore the

blouse to a party the following weekend. Although she was a little uncomfortable in this new attire, she was amazed by the almost magnetic effect it had on several of the male guests. It wasn't long before Eleanor had a new wardrobe with a lot more dash.

What about you? What's in your closet? Greys, browns, blacks, navies; reserved, dignified, dull, boring. . . . This is one chapter where you're not being urged to talk to anybody, to approach anybody, or to call anybody. All you have to do is dress in a way so that people will notice you. Package yourself a little prettier, a bit more colorfully. Have fun with what you wear and you won't fade into the background or be indistinguishable from a piece of furniture. You will be astonished at how successful a simple technique like dressing with more flair can be. Try it!

10

Go Where You're Comfortable

IF NO one's told you yet, you need not go out and suffer. Yet, for some reason shy people view their social lives as an obligatory penance. They stand around in crowded discos, their eyes glued on the clock. When the self-prescribed hour or two is up, they slink out of the place satisfied that at least they have tried.

Books, articles, friends, and relatives are all advising you to go out. Even this very book urges you to go out. But remember, there are many different ways to go out. Make it easy on yourself by going where you feel comfortable.

It's not necessary to force yourself to go to a place that absolutely terrifies you. If you're not comfortable snapping your fingers at a disco, why spend your time being miserable? Singles bars and dances and discos may be fine for some of you but may leave others feeling terribly out of place. So don't go. Go to a place that makes you feel comfortable, a place where you can meet people you can relate to.

Where can you go? You may feel more comfortable at a church- or synagogue-sponsored dance. But you don't need an organized singles gathering to meet. Just use your imagination. What are your interests? What do you like to do with your spare time? Make movies? Watch movies? Ride bicycles? Jog? Fix old cars? Find a group of people, in a club or organization, and attend their gatherings. If you're a passionate amateur photographer, get together with other camera buffs. See what's up on the bulletin board of your local camera shop.

Even if you live in a small town, there are bound to be a few people who share your special interest and, if necessary, a group can be formed that might attract others. That's the nature of society. You will do well by exploiting your pet interests because:

1. *You'll feel comfortable because you are comfortable.* No matter how painfully shy you are, it will be very hard to suppress your natural enthusiasm for, say, tennis. So if you do join a club, you won't want to hang back by the snack shop. No, you'll be right in the middle of things, playing the game you love. It won't be necessary to try to act outgoing. The interest you have in what you are doing will accomplish that for you.

2. *You don't have to put on an act.* There's no prescribed behavior or ritualized conversation to follow when you're doing something you like. Admittedly, in singles bars there most often is, at least at first. But if you love to roller skate, you're going to act *real* out on the floor instead of trying to be what you think might be appropriate for the situation. And speaking of roller skating, it's making a tremendous comeback. Roller rinks and disco roller rinks are popping up all over the place. If you loved skating as a kid give it a try as an adult. A trip to a disco roller rink can be invigorating, fun, and socially rewarding. The atmosphere is easy and relaxed, physical without being hysterical. Single people abound and seem to be meeting with great naturalness and spontaneity.

3. *You're going to meet people who share your interest.* The conversation won't have to be invented. You'll both talk about what you're interested in—the same thing. Think of it. All those

people talking about Indian cooking are your type of people. Gourmet cooks. You can even have each other over to dinner. If you love to ride, take part in all the activities at the local riding academy. You're going to meet people on your wavelength whether you play softball or gaze at the stars or show prize dogs or write poetry.

Jeanine is a young chemist who loves to take ballet lessons. Two nights a week after work and on Saturday mornings she rushes to dance class. One week a good-looking young man showed up in class. It turned out he was a professional ice skater who had been advised to take ballet to develop certain muscles in his legs he would need for more advanced leaps and spins. So there he was standing behind Jeanine at the ballet barre. They went out for coffee one evening after class and pretty soon she was helping him with his ballet and he was teaching her how to ice skate.

No deep interest is too mundane to exploit, nor too specialized to use as a vehicle for meeting new people. Are you reading this and thinking, "That sounds great, but I have no interests." That's impossible; you're not thinking hard enough. Even if all you like to do is knit, you can offer your services to a charity or a hospital and get active in their groups. You only like to read? Join a literary group of people who read and discuss, or take a literature course in night school. You can also do the following:

1. Develop an interest. Is there something you've always wanted to do or learn? Skiing, tennis, swimming, pottery-making? Take the lessons and do it.
2. Go where the "vibes" are right. Many people today are after a more natural, honest life style so they join health clubs or participate in yoga groups or get together to work on self-improvement. It's the age of physical fitness and good karma and you're bound to feel comfortable with these open, friendly types of people.

3. Get involved in politics. If there's some local or national candidate you are enthused about, get involved in some way in their campaign. Even if you lick stamps or make phone calls, you'll be mixing and mingling with all kinds of people.

Don't limit yourself to one group, club, or activity. Do as much as you feel comfortable doing. When you're with people you feel comfortable and at ease with, you'll feel safe. Just remember this: EVEN THE NOT-SO-SHY CAN'T MEET AND MINGLE WHEN THEY DON'T FEEL COMFORT-ABLE.

They have to rely on certain social skills to carry them through. You'll acquire these skills in time, sooner than you think, but it's not necessary now to punish yourself with routine bar-hopping and heavy singles mingles if these kinds of activities turn you off. You will just be serving time and will go home feeling defeated. Leave the bars to people who like to drink and smoke and chat; leave the discos to people who really like to dance. If you're not comfortable, don't go. But, do go someplace where you *are* comfortable.

11

Unexpected Places to Meet People

MANY SHY people, male and female, complain that the competitive tension in places such as discos, singles bars, and parties makes it impossible for them to feel at ease and relaxed. In such a state of anxiety they are unable to start a conversation or approach an attractive stranger.

In the last chapter it was suggested that rather than torture yourself at a singles function you go where you feel comfortable. Listed in this chapter are several unexpected places and situations in which to meet people; situations you'll find yourself in everyday and where you may feel infinitely more comfortable and spontaneous than in traditional singles environments. And these unexpected, often overlooked meeting places are especially ideal for a shy person. In these places and situations everybody has their social guard down, competitive instincts are at a minimum, and people are always less suspicious, a trifle more accepting. You just have to be pleasant and friendly and willing to talk.

In the unexpected places you don't ned a formal introduction to meet someone. He or she may be pinching cantaloupes next to you in the supermarket or sorting socks atop the adjacent dryer at the laundromat or waiting for the same commuter bus as you. Once you open your eyes and recognize that virtually every situation you're in each day has social potential, you'll discover many more available companions.

JUST BROWSING

If you're in a bookstore or a record shop and someone standing nearby looks more interesting than what's on the racks, merely point to the book or record he or she is examining and ask if it's the artist's newest release? What were the reviews like? Suggest your own preferences as well—this is a quick way to find out a lot about someone, his or her tastes, interests, etc.

FRIENDLY INSTRUCTION

In virtually any type of store you will often find a perplexed shopper unable to locate exactly what he or she is looking for. Whether you're an expert on the store's merchandise or a first time visitor, you can offer some advice or assistance. Rarely will you find a person who is unwilling to share conversation with someone who has just offered him or her a helping hand.

Deirdre likes to visit a sport and hobby shop near the harbor in Baltimore. Her father, a seasoned angler, had taught her the fine art of fishing when she was a child. There is hardly a man who can resist Deirdre when she approaches them at the shop to offer advice on a new type of salt-water bait or power reel. She's learned to use her fishing expertise as a way to get around her shyness.

THE EMPTY SEAT

You're in a restaurant or you're getting on a bus, or you're attending a lecture, concert, or movie. If there's an empty seat next to someone you'd love to meet, don't hesitate to ask if the seat is taken—a most natural question. Have no fear, your romantic expectations are *not* written all over your face. Take your time, and when you're ready, start a conversation about anything that seems appropriate: the food, the long commute, the movie, the performer, etc.

CHECK IT OUT

You're wheeling your cart up to the counter at the grocery store. You spot someone very attractive on line. You glance at their cart and find no baby food or Pampers. It looks just like your cart . . . food for one. It takes little ingenuity to think up a conversation opener for a fellow consumer. Just talk about the difficulty of preparing a good meal that isn't too expensive, or whatever else strikes you as sounding concerned and knowledge-able, and like you'd be a willing listener for someone with similar interests.

HERE'S TO YOUR HEALTH

Health nuts aren't so nuts these days. Health clubs, spas, and health food stores seem to be everywhere. Whether you work out at a gym, belong to a health club, or buy your health food supplies somewhere special, you're going to see people there with whom you automatically have something in common. These people share your same vibes. Anything from the excercise program they're on to their favorite vitamin supplement is ideal food for conversation.

LONG WAIT

Long lines can be irritating but they are ready-made situations for conversation. Think of all the times you've stood in line at the bank or post office with nothing to do. Put your time to good use by striking up a conversation with a fellow sufferer. People love to complain in company so you'll have little to do to get them started.

PEDAL POSSIBILITIES

One of the least likely but most incredibly fruitful meeting opportunities for single people is a bicycle tour. These are becoming so popular that classified sections of many papers are filled with weekend tours organized by individuals, groups, and cycling organizations. All you need is your bicycle.

The camaraderie on these trips is spontaneous and natural and many people find that sharing a physical experience like a bike tour is exciting and can also be romantic. Conversation, even intimate exchanges, are easily initiated and very natural during the course of a leisurely bike trip over soft terrain. If you're in decent physical shape and a bike tour sounds appealing to you, don't hesitate to sign up for one.

FLEA MARKETS

What better location to meet single men and women than at a place where they all go to buy inexpensive furniture, clothes, and other knick-knacks. Single people shopping at flea markets are usually interested in finding out about new and creative ways of decorating their recently acquired apartments. Even your most off-hand or unusual suggestion will get a friendly conversation going. You can find a readily available list of garage sales and flea markets in your local newspaper every week.

LECTURES

Churches, schools, government agencies, and various interest groups and organizations all sponsor lecturers and discussions on different subjects. Lectures are especially good unexpected places to meet people, because, in an educational or intellectual atmosphere, people seem unthreatened and unsuspicious of others, even strangers. Lectures are usually well-publicized around town, either in your local paper or newsletter, and there are enough of them so you won't have to travel far.

If you attend a lecture on a subject you're interested in, you'll find people there with whom you share something in common. Be sure to get to the lecture hall early so you can spot that special person in the audience who looks interesting, and then move in close. The lecture topic gives you a built-in conversation opener. While you'll probably have to keep your conversation to a minimum during the lecture, there is plenty of time before and after to get to know a fellow lecture-lover better.

Too many people, shy and otherwise, pass up the lecture circuit because they don't believe they'll meet anyone worth knowing. The thought of attending a lecture fills them with boredom, inertia. This is a mistake. Even if you have to drag yourself out of the house to get there, you'll find that lectures are often not only fascinating and mind-opening, but that they are ideal arenas for meeting attractive and vital men and women.

FOR WOMEN: A MARTIAL ARTS COURSE

If you're interested in this sort of thing and in getting into good physical shape, there's hardly anything that beats a martial arts course for meeting men. Women in these classes are somewhat of a novelty and male classmates seem enchanted by them. There's something about a woman who is capable of roughing up men that elicits a great amount of respect and admiration from them. And don't worry about meeting only muscle men or mindless hulks. Men in the martial arts tend to be much more sensitive, gentle, and intelligent than the average Joe on the street.

Another benefit of a martial arts course is that it builds confidence and inner strength, qualities that will carry over into all aspects of your life, social or otherwise.

FOR MEN: BALLET, KNITTING, OR COOKING CLASSES

Don't knock it until you've tried it. A man who expresses enough interest in ballet or cooking or knitting to join a class full of women, is a man that women will admire. Not only will you become more culturally or domestically aware, but you will also have an opportunity to meet many potential companions.

And shy men will not have to worry for a minute about their shyness. In a class full of women you will undoubtedly be the center of attention and conversation. Just let yourself relax and enjoy the company.

FOR WOMEN: BUSINESS COURSES AND STOCK MARKET CLASSES

Despite an increase in the number of successful businesswomen, classes on business, finance, and investment are still predominantly attended by males. The woman who finds her way into these classes is instantly a curious and exciting attraction among her male classmates. Just like a woman in a martial arts course, the woman in a business course is a captivating addition to the heavily male atmosphere, an unexpected pleasure and the center of much attention.

Of course, there are many more unexpected places to meet people—in fact, every place is a setting in which to start conversation with an attractive stranger. If you are able to recognize the possibilities, the whole world can become your own, non-threatening singles function at which you can meet people. No one will know what you're up to, and, when you're successful, as you often will be, no one will really care.

12

How to Project Positive Body Language

BODY LANGUAGE. Like so many modern phrases that have been absorbed into our language, it is now a cliché. Everybody's heard of it, but do you know exactly what it means?

Body language means communication. It means what your body says about you—whether you intended it that way or not. For your purposes, there is no need to discuss the in-depth psychological interpretations of crossed legs, crossed arms, crossed eyes; you need to know how to make body language work for you.

For shy people, body language can become a sort of delightful disguise. Masked in the handsome armor of positive body language shy people can venture into virtually any social situation and appear cool, confident, and collected—*they can act unshy!*

Several years ago when actress Diane Keaton (the heroine of

the movie *Annie Hall* and many other successful films) was just beginning to emerge as a superstar, she appeared on a late-night talk show. Everyone in the audience was amazed to find that this lovely young woman sat like a gangling adolescent boy, stumbled, blushed, and looked at the floor. She seemed painfully shy. Somehow everyone expected a little more; a movie star is allowed to be a little nervous, but she is supposed to be self-assured, polished, and poised as well. One got the impression, "Gee, she's like me. In fact, she's worse than me . . . and she's a movie star!"

Today when Diane Keaton appears on a talk show she sits up straight, answers questions directly, and looks like a person who feels confident and good about herself. Her body language once said, "I don't think I'm worthy of all this." Now her body language conveys how good she feels about herself. She has grown, matured, and learned to act unshy. Perhaps inside she still feels unworthy, inadequate. It makes no difference. On the outside she appears confident and self-satisfied, and those who watch her respond accordingly.

Too bad you can't walk around holding a mirror and a tape recorder. If you could it would be a lot easier to see how to project positive body language. It is sometimes difficult to distinguish between times when you are projecting positive body language and times when people appear interested only because they're being polite.

Because you don't always receive feedback from other people, or because you are too shy to interpret it properly, the path to mastering positive body language might seem long and difficult at first. In addition to talking, walking, sitting, and standing in "positive" ways, you will also have to be your own objective observer and instructor. You will have to evaluate your performance and make the necessary changes. But after a while, and without quite realizing you're making a breakthrough, you will begin to get a natural "feel" for it.

In the process of developing positive body language, you will invariably make mistakes and achieve mastery in only one aspect at a time. But you should try to keep the whole positive picture in mind. Like any other learning process, the one for positive body language involves diligence and practice. But it is very rewarding. Here are some basic steps toward acquiring positive body language.

ARE YOU SMILING ENOUGH?

What's your mouth doing now? Has it fallen somewhere down around your chin? You can lift the spirits of yourself and others by simply projecting a big, bright smile. Don't, of course, do it inappropriately. Wait for an opening in a conversation or listen to what the persons you're talking to are saying, and smile at their fun, folly, forgetfulness, or whatever. Relate a story or anecdote of your own, and tell it with a genuine, friendly smile. Just as every sentence must end with a period you can dot your own conversation with a smile.

After you become very good at this, you will eventually learn to use your smile to seduce. Yes, a smile can do that. Smiles are very powerful. Ellen is an art director working in Manhattan. There was never a better art director, nor as shy a one. One Friday afternoon Ellen came to the office visibly shaking. She had a date for that night with an extremely handsome and intelligent fellow in her drama class. Despite a ten-minute crash course in positive body language Ellen left the office a nervous wreck.

The following Monday, contrary to what was expected, Ellen came in looking happier than she'd been in months. When queried about her date, she reported that at first she was too nervous and shy to talk. All through dinner she felt like an idiot, mortified by her own silence, only able to smile and nod.

To Ellen's surprise, after she was finishing her chicken parmigiana, her date looked up at her seductively and said, "You have such a terrific smile." This little bit of encouragement was all Ellen needed to open up, and as she and her friend strolled in the moonlight later in the evening, she felt romantic vibrations.

ARE YOUR EYES DIRECTED TOWARD THE OTHER PERSON'S FACE?

This is a difficult thing for shy people to do. They worry that directing their gaze at another person will cause that person to stare back—an unnerving thing for the shy. If this is your fear, try a little trick. Focus your gaze a little bit below or between the person's eyes. As your physical distance from the other person increases, you can even look at their mouth, neck, shoulders. Rest assured that he or she can't tell that you're not actually looking directly in their eyes (try this on a friend). Ask yourself from time to time, "Where are my eyes?" Has your gaze drifted (out of habit) onto the floor or out the window? If it has, the person you're speaking with will feel you're not listening to him. You don't like to feel ignored and neither does anyone else.

As you become more skilled in conversation, you will become so absorbed that eye contact will just happen naturally. You will be able to look directly into the other person's eyes without even being conscious that you are doing it.

ARE YOU STANDING, SITTING, AND WALKING STRAIGHT?

Ramrod straight is not necessary. Just keep reminding yourself not to slump or slouch. When you're alone practice good posture, even if it means putting a book on your head. From that base will come the means by which to move your head, arms, and legs naturally. Even your voice projects better when your posture is good. You'll feel better about yourself and others will notice it. In the beginning you will have to constantly remind yourself to adjust your posture, unless you're a former marine. If you want to watch really good posture, look for movie footage of royalty, or politicians and their wives. These people, who constantly have to impress the public, know the benefits of good posture. So stand up straight. Sit up straight. Walk tall. It says so much about you as a positive person.

Jack knows this to be true. He was at a writer's convention last year, where he related an interesting story. He said that in his job as a publishing executive he felt in a rut. A friend suggested that he try to project a more positive image. So Jack bought a handbook on projecting positive body language and put the suggestions to work.

About a month after he learned the "positive" techniques, Jack said, they had become natural, part of his appearance. One night he went to a party, something he used to do with great nervousness because he was shy around women. He was standing in a corner nursing his rye and ginger ale when an elegant, sophisticated woman with long blonde hair approached. She told Jack that she had spotted him across the room and had to meet him because anyone who stood as straight and looked as aristocratic as he did must be famous. Jack was amused, not to mention flattered and thrilled. They talked all night and dated for a year.

WHAT DO YOU SOUND LIKE?

A strange question. Only other people can really *hear* you. But you can listen to the *sound* of your voice. Does it sound too monotonous? Is it too soft? Is it too high? Is it practically silent? Does it sound too abrupt? When you're alone you can switch on a tape recorder and listen to what your voice sounds like to other people. You can work on lowering a high-pitched, nervous-sounding voice, practice talking a little faster or slower, and make sure you articulate so that others can understand you. Learn to listen to the sound of your voice.

CAN YOU TOUCH SOMEONE NATURALLY?

Have you ever thought of touching someone in conversation? Are you *able* to? It can be done very naturally: "I'm so glad you picked this restaurant," and your hand moves to the other person's arm briefly. Obviously, you won't do this with everybody and not all the time. But you'll probably find that it happens one day quite naturally, as an outgrowth of a more positive you. Remember when someone last touched you affectionately or playfully? It probably made you feel very good, closer to that person. Well, it can have the same effect for you.

HOW IS YOUR HANDSHAKE?

When you greet someone with a handshake, be sure your hand acts as your private diplomat. It should say, "I'm happy to see you." A "cold fish" handshake can be interpreted as rejection or even dislike. So (without becoming a human vise) put a lot of energy into a handshake. A good handshake is positive.

Perhaps you have a stuttering problem, you blush, or you get the shakes. These annoying little symptoms of your shyness probably cause you untold embarrassment and pain. But they are not unusual symptoms and not nearly as obvious as you imagine. At any rate, projecting positive body language will help these symptoms to fade away.

Here is your positive body language homework. Some of you may have mastered most of the following techniques already. For others, your shyness body language may be so ingrained that you'll have to clean your slate and start from the beginning.

- Remember to relax your mouth with a smile as often as possible.

- Don't let your eyes say shy: Look at the other person during conversation.
- Sit up straight.
- Walk tall.
- Listen to the sound of your own voice while you are talking.
- Shake hands firmly and positively.
- Touch someone in the course of conversation, when the time seems appropriate, or when it comes from your heart.

The perception of those who seem shy and those who don't is often the result of a superficial gesture, a look, or a tone of voice. Imagine being introduced to twins at a party. One looks you directly in the eye and smiles. The other glances at the floor, shuffles his feet, and slouches. Even if the twins were identical in personality you would assume the former to be friendly and outgoing, the latter to be awkward and shy, only because one looked you directly in the eye and stood up tall and the other didn't.

Think of this little example in relation to yourself. Simply by learning to adopt the body language of the unshy, you can *appear* confident. And get people to respond to you in kind. Sometimes the beginning of a warm, loving relationship can be the result of a single, simple movement—a smile, a direct look, an uncomplicated mechanical procedure you can master in a few days. And that in a nutshell is why positive body language is so worthwhile mastering.

13

How to Detect Positive Body Language

THERE IS more to positive body language than simply learning to use it. For the shy person, learning to detect positive body language in others is also important.

Shy people are often so self-conscious that they do not notice when someone approaches them with interest or affection. Every day people use their bodies (their smile, their touch, their eyes, etc.) to tell you they like you. By learning to read and detect these body language "hints," you will discover that many more people than you ever suspected are drawn to you.

Here are the major bodily "hints" to look for in others:

WATCH THE EYES

When someone is speaking or listening to you, does she (or he) look you directly in the eyes? "Shifty-eyed" characters, people who glance away frequently, those who talk to you while staring at a chair, are either terribly shy themselves, insincere, or not interested in you. Consider this scenario: You're sitting over dinner in an elegant restaurant with an attractive companion. With meaning and honesty she says in a seductive voice, "I've never met anyone quite like you. You're the most wonderful person I've ever known." It all sounds terribly romantic, until you realize that the other person is glancing about the room while that flattering gem is being directed your way.

On the other hand, if someone whispers romantic things while gazing deeply and enchantedly into your eyes, you can be pretty sure he is being honest and sincere. (Note: Beware of aspiring actors or actresses. For them every encounter is dramatic.)

If you're in a singles bar or discotheque, or at a party, and you notice a gaze directed your way, stay in the line of vision. If the person who's looking at you glances over more than once, this is almost always a nonverbal invitation. When you attract someone's interest repeatedly, this means you are pleasing to her (or his) eyes. Work your way closer until it's somewhat comfortable to address her with a conversation opener. If you can't think of anything to say, use one of the opening lines or snatchers of small talk listed in this book. You'll discover that a lot more people have been looking you over with romance in mind than you ever realized. It's essential to alert you to this because shy people often misinterpret other's darting glances as critical. A shy person may think "I know why she (or he) is looking at me like that. She can see I'm different, uncomfortable, and shy." It's possible that this is what your observer is thinking, but it's improbable. People soon ignore what they find odd or distasteful. It's much more likely that those eyes you feel looking you up and down are admiring you.

WATCH THE MOUTH

A smile is one of the greatest things to give and receive and it costs nothing. True, there are some people who never stop smiling (a used-car salesman or your banker), and at times it can seem phony and insincere. But, for the most part, when someone smiles at you, it means he likes something about you. As you become more experienced in detecting body language, you'll be able to distinguish a genuine, personal smile from a phony or courteous smile. Another person's smile can be used as a barometer to measure interest in you. And, like eye contact, a genuine smile is often an invitation for you to move closer. So watch for smiles. They *mean* something.

LOOK AT BODY POSITION

Sometimes, without realizing it themselves, people use subtle shifts in body posture to show interest in others. You'll notice at a bar or party, when two people are talking romantically, that their bodies naturally move closer and lean toward each other.

Watch talk show hosts like Dick Cavett or Merv Griffin. By simply moving their upper bodies closer to a nervous guest they can make that person feel more at ease, more comfortable.

People always use this simple gesture as a nonverbal message that says, "I'm interested in you," or "I like to be near you." Be aware of a person's body position. If you sense someone inching closer, it's an unmistakable sign he wants to be close to you. Again, it's important to alert you to this because shy people often overlook such indicators, so caught up are they with thoughts of what a negative impression they're making.

LOOK FOR TOUCH

"Touchers" can be annoying if they *never* let you alone. Too many elbow tweaks, too many arm pats, an excess of hugging—it can make you feel uncomfortable. But that's the exception. Most of the time a toucher is balm to the soul, not to mention the body. Gentle touching and subtle body contact can be very exciting. And make no mistake, when someone starts leaning forward to pat your knee or touch your arm, it almost always means exactly what you suspect it does. Another nice thing about touchers is that they are usually physical people who enjoy contact, who feel free to use their bodies. If you're shy and you meet someone who is repeatedly touching you, like a teddy bear, realize this is probably a sign that they like you, are attracted to you. If you in turn are attracted to them, don't let the coziness of the interchange evaporate. If it feels appropriate, touch the person back as you converse, and keep in mind that if someone feels comfortable enough to spontaneously touch you, chances are he or she is interested in dating you as well.

LISTEN TO THE SOUND OF VOICES

This is not the same as listening to their words. Oftentimes a person can be saying one thing while his body language and specific voice inflection is conveying a totally different message. The person might be smiling, using eye contact, maybe even touching, but the voice is all wrong. Perhaps you detect a touch of agitation or anger, a sharp drop or increase in volume, or a nervous tremor. Everything tells you that the actual communication is somehow different from the content of the words.

When a person is using positive voice inflection, she (he) talks at the appropriate volume with the appropriate intonation. She uses appropriate words. What she is saying sounds natural, fluid, and smooth. When you develop an ear for it, the sound of a person's voice can tell you a lot about her or his intentions.

OBSERVE FRIENDS AND ACQUAINTANCES

You can begin to develop the skills of detecting messages in body language by observing the friends, co-workers, and strangers you see everyday. Does your lab partner, who you're sure has more dates than she can handle, keep glancing at you during biology?

And what about the librarian who smiled so warmly at you for no apparent reason? And the man you see at the bus stop each morning. Is it just your imagination, or does his leaning toward you *mean* something?

Once you begin to read the true messages that come from body language, you will discover that dozens of acquaintances feel a whole lot closer to you than you realized. During those times when you're feeling just a little nervous and uncomfortable, it's good to know that others are giving you hundreds of nonverbal cues to help you along. And learning to detect positive body language in others will go a long way toward helping you project positive body language of your own.

14

Tuning in to Assertiveness

You're a young guy just entering the business world. You're quite intelligent and not unattractive, but very shy. After settling in New York and discovering a delightful pub just two blocks from your apartment, you think you finally might meet someone to love, or at least to like. On Friday night you put on your best clothes and head down to the pub. After one drink you're feeling good and confident and you approach an attractive blonde at the bar. "Hi. I'm new to New York," you say. "Is this bar always so popular?"

To your amazement the blonde turns and smiles and you begin talking about the neighborhood, the sights, good vacation spots on Long Island, and so on. You're feeling comfortable and enjoying yourself more than you have in quite some time. Then a good-looking, macho type strolls over and asks the girl you're with how she's doing. In two minutes he has his arm around her

FRIEND (as PAUL): I've really enjoyed seeing you, Susan. You're very attractive and very friendly.

SUSAN: Thank you, Paul, those are nice compliments. I like you too.

FRIEND: We've been seeing quite a lot of each other. You really turn me on. After dinner why don't we go up to my place for a little wine and soft music.

SUSAN: That sounds very romantic, Paul. But I'm not ready for that. Maybe we could just go for a walk in the park or maybe to a movie.

FRIEND: Listen, Susan, we don't have to go to bed. I just want to hold you and enjoy being close to you. We've been seeing each other for weeks—you can trust me.

SUSAN: I really do like you, Paul, but I don't want to put myself in the position of having to turn you down. Maybe when we know each other better and I feel more comfortable with you . . .

FRIEND: Susan, I've taken you to expensive restaurants and to the theater. I wouldn't have spent a lot of money on you if I really didn't like you. Going to bed is just a natural ending to a pleasant evening.

SUSAN: Paul, I've enjoyed our dates a lot and I'm sure you sincerely like me. But going to bed with a man just because we've dated isn't natural for me.

FRIEND: I don't know why you're so against it. Every girl I date goes to bed with me. It's not a sin.

SUSAN: Paul, I'm sorry if you feel offended, but I guess I'm not like every girl you date, and I'm not interested in going to bed with you now.

FRIEND: Well, you sure are stubborn, but if that's how you feel I'll drop it.

SUSAN: Thanks, I'm glad you understand.

Susan was afraid that Paul might react angrily to her assertive refusal to sleep with him, so she role-played several other scenes until she felt comfortable in all of them. The next time Susan

and she's laughing excitedly. You stand around for a
feeling hurt, and finally leave the bar sulking and defeate

You're a twenty-five-year-old legal secretary living in a
of Miami. One of the other women in the office asks y
party on Friday night. Although you're dreadfully shy,
anxious to meet new men and accept the invitation. At t
you get a drink and sit on a chair in a corner. Several
talking when two attractive men walk in. The hostess in
the men to the other girls but neglects to introduce you.
hurt, but just keep sitting in the corner and don't s
Later, other guests start dancing while you stare at albu
You finally leave the party dejected and disappointed.

Sound familiar? These are just two of many similar s
people tell. Very few shy people realize they have cer
that must be respected by other people. Shy people co
while others could rightfully expect certain things fr
they hardly ever expected the same things in return f
people. Shy people constantly find themselves h
situations where their rights are being violated, es
social situations. At these times, when the shy pe
fidence and assertive abilities are usually low, he or
particularly vulnerable to violations from other peop

Many psychologists believe that Assertiveness Tr
can be tremendously helpful in conquering shynes
the case of Susan for instance. While she enjoyed t
she had with Paul, she felt he was getting too person
Susan feared that Paul would ask her to go to bed, so
didn't want to do at that early stage in their relati
complained that her shyness prevented her from
Paul's advances, and that she would probably end
bed with him as she had done unwillingly with ot!

Susan was told that while her shyness was inde
in this case what she was really suffering from wa:
of assertiveness. She role-played, or acted out, wi
assertiveness approach to dealing with Paul's ac
some practice here's how it finally went:

went out with Paul he did ask her up to his room, and she commenced with the dialogue as she had role-played it. It went even better than planned. Susan reported that Paul told her he respected her for being so firm with him. He told her that so many women go to bed with men on the first date these days that he really respected a woman who refused. Paul and Susan dated for three more months before they did go to bed. Susan said it was a wonderful experience and it left her feeling good about herself, a welcome change from her past affairs.

Susan continued a program of Assertiveness Training. After a few weeks she not only was handling her social life assertively, but she reported that by using assertiveness she could control her shyness in business situations as well. She's been looking more confident and happy than she has in years. Susan commented recently, "I can't believe how easy and fun it is to be assertive . . . and I'm shy!"

Life is like a tug-of-war. In every interpersonal experience we have there is give and take, push and pull. Unfortunately, when shy people are pushed, manipulated, or exploited, they usually don't push back or even try to stand their ground. Too often shy people (because they are also unassertive) do things they don't want to do and as a result both their self-respect and self-esteem suffer.

Contrary to what many people think, assertiveness is not aggression. *Aggressive* people try to manipulate others in order to get what they want, even at the expense of another person's rights. *Assertive* people express their feelings and needs and defend their legitimate rights without violating the rights of others. Assertive people are honest and direct when expressing themselves and are not intimidated by the behavior of others. Assertiveness Training teaches shy people the skills involved in relating to people around them in all situations: in business, at home, wherever they are interacting with others.

Why has AT been so effective for shy people? Because, like this book, AT involves action. AT does not spend lots of time analyzing why you are shy. Instead, it teaches you how to immediately begin dealing with your shy behavior. When shy people begin to act assertively, honestly and directly, and stand up for their rights, then their confidence is increased, they begin to feel comfortable in all interpersonal situations, their self-respect grows, and the gnawing fears associated with their shyness, that they've been suffering from for years, disappear quickly.

Very often just the mere act of telling a shy person to recognize certain rights and stand up for them helps them to begin acting assertively. Shy people must recognize their rights and fight for them. If other people are allowed to manipulate them, then the Shyness Syndrome goes into effect . . . other people making demands and unreasonable requests of the shy person while he (or she) sits quietly by feeling angry, used, and frustrated, and allowing others to define his (or her) role in all situations.

"Okay," you're saying, "I'm convinced. Assertiveness Training can work for me. Let me have it, I want to be rid of this awful shyness as soon as possible!" Unfortunately, one chapter is not sufficient space to describe a good, thorough, effective AT program. It would be doing you an injustice to try and briefly present an AT program for, in fact, assertiveness taught incompletely can be more hurtful than helpful to the shy person. Often a shy person might find herself confusing aggressive and assertive reactions, or even cornering herself with ill-applied assertiveness.

But there are a few things you can do. If you're feeling stoked up about AT, you can join an Assertiveness Training group. Many towns and certainly every large city has one, and it is the most effective way to learn AT because you learn with other shy and unassertive people. Also, if there is a local college nearby, they probably have a program setup or can tell you where to find one. If you attend college, an assertiveness group is probably no farther away than your counseling center. College health centers have been pushing assertiveness as an effective treatment for all sorts of social problems above and beyond shyness itself. If you just feel too shy to enter one of these groups or talk to a counselor, then you should get a hold of at least one of the many good books written on assertiveness. They are readily available in your library or at your bookstore. Two books that are especially well-written are Dr. Herbert Fensterheim's *Don't Say Yes If You Want to Say No* and Dr. Manuel Smith's *When I Say No, I feel Guilty*. They are both very complete, useful guides to becoming assertive.

If you know someone who is assertive or if you have a friend who is assertive, you may want to take cues from him and give it a try on your own. While this isn't the ideal approach, go ahead if it gets you into action. Try to get someone to role-play with you as Susan did. Difficult situations that involve assertiveness are usually easier to handle if they have been acted out beforehand with a friend or relative. Don't be afraid or embarrassed to use role-playing—it is a very useful tool. If you undertake an assertive program on your own, perhaps with the use of a book, and you have doubts whether a specific act was assertive or not, ask yourself whether it increased your self-respect even slightly. If it did, it was assertive. If not, it was unassertive.

But whichever course of action you decide on, do it! Assertiveness Training can be an effective tool against many of the things that shyness causes you to do, oftentimes against your will. No matter how shy you are, assertiveness will help. And best of all, as it was for Susan, it can be fun.

15

"It Doesn't Feel Right!"

A LOT of things you're being asked to do in this book probably won't feel right, may seem unnatural and awkward, like someone else is going through the motions. You might feel at times it's just not "you" who is practicing to act unshy. This is *not* an excuse to drop the program. Just because some of the exercises seem pointless or phony or not your "style" doesn't mean they won't help.

Randy had a little analogy to underscore this point. Up until several years ago he had what he was convinced was an incurably weak backhand in tennis. Nothing he did with it felt right. He just couldn't hit the ball with any naturalness or comfort. If you asked Randy to predict his future on the tennis courts, he would have looked through the years and seen the same terrible backhand.

As a last resort he followed a friend's advice and signed up for a dozen tennis lessons. It was a special—a dozen lessons for fifty dollars. Although he was positive it was fifty dollars wasted he went to the lessons anyway, but only with the most distant expectation of success. At first, everything the instructor told him to do felt awkward, clumsy, and unnatural. Randy did exactly as he was told, but he knew that while these techniques might work for everyone else, they would never work for him. He felt as if he had a cauliflower in his hand, not a tennis racket.

Then, during his sixth or seventh lesson, something magical happened. He hit one shot and it felt good. The ball flew off the racket straight and true, a flat, hard, cross-court shot. A few strokes later it happened again. And then again. Then it was happening almost all the time and beginning to feel right. Pretty soon he no longer felt clumsy when hitting a backhand. Today the stroke is as natural to Randy as hitting his forehand.

What's the point of all this? At one time Randy felt as awkward hitting a backhand as you may feel making small talk at a party. But almost any new skill takes time to acquire, to feel as if it's part of you. Watch a baby learning to walk. It'll wobble, stumble, fall, cry, pick itself up, start all over again, and soon it's walking as naturally as if it were born walking.

You'll be asked to do things in this book that may feel clumsy and crazy . . . even a little dishonest. You'll say to yourself, "This is insane! I can't do this." You'll think maybe the technique might work for someone else, but not you. The answer to that is that these antishyness exercises *will* work for you. You'll be able to act as unshy as anyone. These exercises may feel funny at first but give them time—two weeks, two months—and before you know it you're going to have a breakthrough, the same way Randy did the day his backhand started to come naturally. And this will lead to the day when you'll feel open and at ease with all kinds of people, be able to go to parties and have fun, to make dates and woo lovers with ease and comfort. And it will all come naturally.

So even though it might not feel right for you at the beginning, make a leap of faith and plunge into these techniques. No matter how awkward and uncomfortable you might feel, do them anyway. For even though you may not notice that you're making progress, you will be. And a short time later, much sooner than you expected, something magical will happen. We're absolutely sure of it.

16

Your First Step Toward Success

ACTION, NOT contemplation, is the key to conquering shyness. Most how-to books are written on the premise that by philosophizing, theorizing, and analyzing about problems, a cure will somehow mystically follow. Nonsense! That is the worst way for people to learn to act unshy.

Shy people as a rule tend to be too analytical to begin with. They do a great deal of—"I wonder if I should have said . . ." or, "I wonder if that person's thinking I'm. . . ." Shy people spend more time "contemplating their navels" than taking any useful action to help themselves. It's part of the whole Shyness Syndrome. Consequently, this is not a book that helps you indulge your proclivity for contemplation. It just wouldn't be at all productive.

No, this is a how-to book that emphasizes action and practical application. That's the only way you're going to learn to overcome your symptoms of shyness and start living and loving the way you'd like.

Here is the first step you're being asked to take:

Tomorrow, or even today if you're reading this over your morning coffee, go up to someone to whom you're reasonably attracted and speak with him for up to three but not more than five minutes.

No, it cannot be your mother or father or anyone like that. That would not have any beneficial effect in helping you overcome your shyness.

Yes, it should be someone you're fairly familiar with. Not a complete stranger but somebody you're acquainted with at work or school, or wherever you spend most of your day.

Do you have to be madly in love with the person? No. Just interested. Make it someone you think you might like to know better. But it should not be a man who makes you feel weak in the knees, speechless everytime he passes by. Nor should it be that gorgeous woman in the next office who scares the living daylights out of you. It must be someone you think you can talk to for five minutes.

Do you have to ask for a date?

Absolutely not. (Of course, you can accept an invitation if it's offered, but that's *not* your goal.) Don't even ask for the person's phone number. ALL YOU HAVE TO DO IS SPEND THREE TO FIVE MINUTES IN CONVERSATION WITH THE PERSON.

Now, you're wondering, *talk about what?* Well, here's the kicker. You don't actually have to try to talk about anything, because here is what you're going to do: ASK FOR ADVICE.

Asking people for advice invariably draws them into conversation with you. People *love* to give advice. What kind of advice can you ask for? Well, if you ask for the time, your conversation will be under a quarter of a minute. The person will respond with something like, "Wait a second. Oh, yeah, it's a quarter to three." On the other hand, if you approach someone who has a digital watch, admire it, ask how it works, and where he got it—well, you'll probably have to excuse yourself to keep the conversation from going over five minutes.

But if you charge up and ask someone whether or not she thinks you should get a second opinion on an upcoming operation, or something equally personal, that might easily turn the person off.

Also, timing is fairly important. If you clearly see that the person you want to approach is in the midst of having the worst day of her life, or is frazzled and busy and very irritable, wait for a better opportunity. That person is not going to be receptive. But don't fool yourself or procrastinate by imagining that the person you want to talk to is always too busy. It would be better to choose another person than wait too long.

Asking for advice is the easiest icebreaker. Here is a list of ten tried and true subjects to ask advice about. Some may come in handy for your arsenal of topics. Others may seem silly or way-out. You probably will feel more comfortable with one that's entirely your own and fits the person and situation. Nevertheless, here are some sample questions:

- My folks are coming into town this weekend. Can you recommend any good restaurants?
- I'm thinking of getting a new stereo. What kind of system do you have?
- I'm thinking of buying a new car. How do you like yours?
- I heard you went to Aruba on your vacation. How was the snorkeling down there?
- Where can you jog around here without getting hit by a car?
- How's that new place that just opened for lunch?
- I noticed you're reading *Separate Vacations*. Is it as sexy as it sounds?
- I saw you coming out of Gessner's scriptwriting course. Is it worth taking?
- You look like you understood that lecture. Can you explain transcendentalism to me?

- You sure have lost weight. How did you do it?
- I notice you've started wearing contact lenses. Don't they hurt?

The above will give you an *idea* of what kind of advice to ask for. If you can think of a juicier topic—"Hey, Joe, are you going to quit if the company merges or do you think it's worth staying on?" or "I understand you took Logic with Professor X. I heard that course was impossible. What do you think?"—so much the better.

If you already are quite familiar with the person you're planning on asking for advice, be very aware of working a mutual or special interest into the conversation. If you know the person brings his tennis racket to work or school and plays at lunch, there's an obvious opening. On the other hand, it would be ludicrous to ask someone who doesn't drive where to get the best deal on a used car. Look for the question that will strike a chord in the particular person you're going to approach, something the person will want to stop and talk about for three to five minutes. He will feel flattered that you sought him out for advice.

You can wear a watch or glance at a wall clock and time yourself. Remember, you don't have to talk any longer than three minutes. You end it by graciously thanking the person you approached for her advice, excusing yourself with something like, "Well, I really have to be getting back to (whatever)."

Now, there will be some of you who are going to think this exercise is simple. Well, if you have advanced to that stage—wonderful. And that's not said to be sarcastic. You will have less work to do than the terribly shy, but you still have plenty of work ahead of you, so do this simple exercise anyway. This is a program, and like anything that is well thought out it runs from an A point all the way to a Z point. So you might as well do A and enjoy A, because if you think A is a cinch—it's going to get more challenging.

There will be others who find the exercise intriguing. A

sensible chore. If that's the case don't think any more about it than that. Just do it.

Still others are going to find it horrendously difficult. Well, if that's how you feel, you've got to try it anyway. You bought this book for it to help you, and it was written to help you. If you follow the exercises and keep plugging away, you will have a better social life and a whole new attitude about life in general. If you're going to just read it and study the theories, you'd be advised to read the other kind of how-to book, the "nonaction" type book. It won't make as many demands on you. It won't ask you to take risks. And it will not pester you out of your shyness by continually suggesting ways for you to get out and do something.

You can find people to talk to, to date, to kiss, to hug, to love, to dance with, to hold your hand, to share your bed, to get engaged to, to marry. Just try the techniques.

Try this first exercise and all the rest that come along. They're not meant to be tedious or terrifying. The reward comes in the fun of what happens when you accomplish them. For those of you who might have to reach beyond yourself—do it. That's sometimes what getting over your shyness is all about. It takes a little guts. But it's worth it.

Don't be negative. If you call the wrong shot the first time (the person can't give you advice and the conversation ends as if you had asked for the time of day), *don't* give up. Try again. And again if (although unlikely) you have to. By asking people for their advice, you are asking them something about themselves. And people love to talk about themselves. They are going to warm up to you. Give it a try. Soon.

17

Don't Pull Out the Package

RAY IS a thirty-year-old copywriter in an ad agency. He's a very talented, creative person, and, as often goes along with those traits, sensitive and extremely shy too. Occasionally he does manage to drag himself to a party or a bar with a few close friends. And oftentimes, because he is cute in a boyish kind of way, women will approach him and start chatting. Ray acts nervous, somewhat embarrassed, but he generally begins to loosen up and have a good time.

He will drink, dance, chat about work, smile, and laugh. Then, suddenly, he does something that he knows is wildly self-destructive but he just can't seem to help himself. To the surprise, dismay, and disappointment of his new acquaintance, he *pulls out the package.* Just when the woman is getting turned on to him, he feels an overwhelming need, a driving compulsion to confess his shyness and sensitivity. He tells whatever girl he's met how difficult it is for him to go to parties, how he never really feels comfortable with women, how he practically had a nervous breakdown when his last relationship broke off, and how he couldn't go out for six months because of it. And on and on and on. He simply cannot stop himself.

Think of the poor woman he has cornered. All she did was spot a good-looking guy, gear herself up to make an approach, happily found that she was enjoying herself, and then, *boom*, from nowhere she's getting her ear bent. She starts to think, "Who needs this guy?"

Ray was not in need of analysis and he wasn't crazy. He just had this compulsion to tell *all* too soon. People have very sensitive antennae and, even unconsciously, shrink away from what seems like unhealthy behavior. To many people, pulling out the package is just that, unhealthy behavior, and it will almost always ruin a promising evening.

Many shy people seem to be compulsive in just this way. Unable to contain themselves, they have to let the other person, a virtual stranger, know exactly who they are. Since shyness is not visible, why pull out the package? When you are meeting someone for the first time, or on a first date, your feelings of shyness are not something they should know about—not at this stage of the game and certainly not in this way.

During the course of a relationship, you can begin to tell someone about your shyness, but to pull out your troubles and travails immediately is practically suicidal.

What shy people are really trying to say is, "Look, I have this rotten flaw. I want you to know now, so you have a chance to back out from knowing me." Or, worse, by pulling out the package they are saying, "See, so after I tell you all this, you'll never want to know me or go out with me and I can just crawl back into my comfortable shell of shyness." In either case it's self-destructive.

What can you do about this habit of "compulsing" your social life right down the drain? Well, there is a solution:

1. Talk about it. No, not to your date. Talk over this urge to tell all with anyone you consider a confidant. Your mother, your

next-door neighbor, your cousin, or your friend. Tell that person you just can't help yourself. You simply have this itching urge to tell a potential date just how shy you are and you do it way too soon. If you try talking the compulsions away, you eventually won't have them anymore. Somehow the physical process of giving voice to it, admitting and recognizing the problem, alleviates it to a great extent. Again, this doesn't mean talking about it to the wonderful new person you met five minutes ago at a party.

2. When you're really tempted to "talk": DON'T SAY ANYTHING. Whether you're at a disco, a party, a bar, or on a moonlit balcony in Pago Pago, when you feel that compulsion coming on, stifle yourself. Whatever you were about to say, just don't say it. If you have to stand and bite your lip in silence, fine. It also might be easier to get over the moment by smiling, smoking a cigarette, popping a stick of gum into your mouth, nursing your drink, or anything else you can think of. But, do not pull out the package.

That very act of not compulsing and confessing your shyness right away will strengthen relationships that used to end all too soon in the past. Ray found out that by keeping his mouth shut on the first date, by the fifth date he could have an interesting discussion about some of his inner feelings without scaring the person away. Even if you are a reformed criminal or have a shady past, all the other person has to know on the first date is that he or she likes you. People judge by what they see. If you made it all the way to the eighth date, and in the course of conversation you revealed that you were painfully shy, your date would say, "Aw, c'mon. *You*."

Pulling out the package can be done very subtly too. One can pull out the package and have it wrapped in pretty, shiny, little boxes. Here's a little scenario you may have participated in at least once in your life:

"Like to dance?"

"Me? No, let's just stand here. I have two left feet. I can't dance. People would stare."

"Hey, c'mon, everyone can dance. I'll teach you. Look, you came here tonight and you knew it was a dance." (*Other person is still kidding around but being helpful.*)

"Oh, that's because I pushed myself out the door. I have the hardest time going places. I'm just, you know, so shy. A person like you doesn't have to worry."

"Well, I have times when I feel uncomfortable." (*Other person is beginning to have second thoughts.*)

"Oh, nothing like me, I bet."

"I dunno." (*looking for an out*) "Oh, look, there's an old friend of mine. Excuse me. Nice meeting you."

Another caution. Sometimes you'll get what seems like a natural invitation to talk about your inner problems. Don't. Someone you bump into at a party might say, "Gee, I hate these affairs. They make me feel so uncomfortable. Shy, too." This is not an open door to pull out the package. They do not mean what they say. What they mean is, "I'm going to utter this cute little icebreaker because I'm nervous." The two of you may have a vastly different interpretation of what it means to be shy. So, in this case, say only, "Oh, yeah, I know what you mean. I feel the same way." Then button up. It's nothing more than a conversation opener.

Do not pull out the package. Your compulsion is nothing more than wanting to eat a whole box of cookies because they're there. When you finish you'll be sorry. Wait until you get to know someone better before you talk about your heartfelt shyness. Then it will have meaning, instead of ruining a potentially good relationship. Pulling out the package says more than you intended. It gives the person the impression that you could be trouble. If you just save the heavy disclosure for later, you'll be making an important step toward acting unshy.

18

What Do You Really Want?

GRETCHEN WAS the sister of a secretary who worked in a talent agency. She was very petite and cute, and with her blonde short-cropped hair and button nose she looked less than her twenty-five years.

Since Gretchen was shy and had trouble meeting men, her sister suggested she come around to the agency in the late afternoon. The agency was always filled with exciting male writers and talent scouts, and Gretchen's sister thought it would be a great way for her to meet guys.

Gretchen was very sweet and sensitive, and it was surprising that men didn't date her. But Gretchen always did a curious thing. While she was at the agency office, she spent her time leafing through the many magazines that were lying around, particularly those with male models. "Oh, this guy is gorgeous. Look at the eyes on this one. Wow, what a body—he must be a surfer. I'd give anything to go out with this guy," she would say. She went on like that for hours, not even noticing the many attractive and friendly guys in the office.

One afternoon Howard, the owner of the agency, approached her. "Gretchen, if you could date any guy you want, who would it be?"

"Oh, wow," she said. "Definitely Robert Redford."

"Robert Redford?" Howard replied, "Really? A relationship with Robert Redford? That's very interesting."

"Oh, no, not a *real* relationship or anything," she hastened to add. "Not with a man like that. I don't think I'd ever feel secure or at ease. I guess I mean it'd just be nice to go to bed with Robert Redford." Gretchen blushed.

"So then you really don't want Robert Redford after all?" Howard asked.

"Oh, no," Gretchen admitted, "I'd be much happier with just a friendly guy who cared about me."

Shy people fantasize so much and so wildly, and their expectations for themselves are so great, that oftentimes they lose touch with their true feelings and sentiments. They become so entangled in the desires of their fantasy lives that they don't know what they really want.

Gretchen's fantasies allowed her to imagine herself with only the most gorgeous of men. When Howard finally asked her what she really wanted, she realized that she would be very happy with the guy next door. She discovered that dating a movie star or male model wasn't really what she wanted at all. Suddenly, she began to notice the males at the agency, and they began to notice her. She stopped visiting her sister's office about a week later, but only after she met and started dating a young, fairly ordinary, but very interesting contract agent.

Chuck's story is similar. A few years ago, he was always talking about one or another beautiful girl who he spotted on the street or who came into his office. He would spend his weekends at singles bars gazing at gorgeous girls, but he never really approached or dated one. He just stared at them with his friends, became discouraged with himself when he never talked to any, and usually would wind up going home alone.

Chuck's problem was a classic case of not knowing what he

really wanted. When asked if he had ever dated a girl seriously, Chuck said no. Then when asked if he was friendly with any girls, he mentioned one, Angela, a teller at his bank.

As he described Angela, Chuck's face seemed to light up, and he became visibly more relaxed. She was not very good-looking, he explained, but she was attractive in her own special way and very friendly. Chuck said he felt comfortable when he talked to her, and he even took her to lunch once. After Chuck described Angela, the matter wasn't mentioned again that day.

About a week later Chuck was asked to draw up a list of characteristics he would like in a girl. He was told to leave out physical attributes. As expected, Chuck's list matched almost identically with the description of Angela he had offered only a few days before. When this was pointed out to him, he seemed shocked. He said he had never thought of dating Angela, but it seemed so obvious now. He didn't know why it had never occurred to him. He had been so caught up in his fantasy expectations he had overlooked a fine, approachable girl.

Chuck asked Angela out that same week. She was thrilled and admitted to Chuck that she had always wanted to be closer to him but didn't know how. At the time of this writing, Chuck and Angela have been living together for eight months and they're now talking about marriage.

The point is simply this. Shy people sometimes lose touch with the reality of their desires. They spend night after night disappointed because they haven't found the god or goddess they've been looking for at a singles bar, and actually all they really want is a pleasant person to go out with and feel close to. They'd be satisfied with someone sweet like the girl who married their brother, or the quiet, polite guy who's dating their roommate.

If you're a shy person who thinks you'll only be satisfied with a glamorous lover, try this suggestion. Take a few minutes and write a list of the qualities you like in a person. Get in touch with your true feelings, not your fantasies. Use the questions below as a guide to drawing a picture of that special person. The list doesn't include physical attributes because it's time you started to be aware of important characteristics other than appearances. Add your own questions to these below. If in two or three months of using it, you change one of your notions about what you really want, change the list accordingly. Ask yourself who you really want:

1. What kinds of interests should she or he have? The same as yours, similar, or completely different?
2. Do you want to date a shy person, a person who's moderately shy, or a socially aggressive individual?
3. If the person smokes or drinks, would that bother you?
4. Should he or she be athletic and love sports?
5. Is it okay if the person has been married before? If she or he has children?
6. What kind of educational background should the person have?
7. Would it bother you if the person had a better, more prestigious job than yours?
8. Would you want someone who was a little sexually naive, a person who was moderately experienced, or someone who was sexually uninhibited?

Expand this list of questions in any way that will help you get a clear picture of what you really want. By realizing that you don't need to have Candice Bergen or John Travolta in order to feel satisfied, you can start to meet and date people who are readily within your reach. Once your expectations for yourself become realistic, you'll see that there are people all around you who want to date and have relationships with you, and these people will meet your needs better than any movie star or model.

When you meet people in the future, look beyond their physical appearances. Use your list to start appraising the character and personality of people. You'll soon be meeting and dating the type of person who you *really* want.

19

Office Superstar, Weekend Loner

SEVERAL YEARS ago, Jack and his wife Vivian got a call from a distant young cousin who had moved to New York. Her name was Cathy. "Why don't I stop by sometime this weekend?" Cathy suggested. And so they invited her for Saturday-morning brunch.

Cathy immediately struck Jack and Vivian as bright, ambitious, and cute. She had a very demanding job as legal secretary for three lawyers plus she was going to law school at night.

After brunch Cathy asked if there was a good hardware store in town. When informed there were several, she sped off in her little orange Fiat and disappeared for several hours. When she returned around three o'clock in the afternoon, she headed into the backyard with a novel and plopped herself down in a garden chair to read. Jack was a little curious. He and Vivian were planning a party for later in the evening. Was his young cousin planning to stay the weekend?

Five o'clock came and then six and still Cathy didn't give the slightest hint that she was leaving. "Listen," Jack said finally, "we're having a party tonight with some friends, mostly married people about our own age. You're perfectly welcome to come, but I think you might find it a little dull."

"No, I won't," said Cathy. "I like people of all ages." And indeed she did. Cathy had a ball at the party chatting with the guests, particularly with one of the women, who was an entertainment lawyer.

The next weekend Cathy dropped by without even calling. "I had to come back and pick up some more screws and bolts at the hardward store, so I thought I'd just stop by for a visit," she explained. Jack noticed she had a little overnight bag with her. The kids were throwing a frisbee around in the backyard and with a happy whoop of recognition Cathy ran out to join them. As you've probably guessed by now, Cathy spent the whole weekend at Jack's house and many of the following ones too.

At first Jack enjoyed playing the role of gracious host to an out-of-town relative. Cathy was bright, pretty, lively, and good company to have around the house. "But why isn't she dating?" Jack wondered. "How come she doesn't seem to have friends of her own age? This isn't natural, an attractive young single girl spending all her free time with older married couples." Jack began to think that perhaps his vivacious young cousin was, underneath it all, shy. And it struck him that if this were the case, he really wasn't doing her much of a favor by making his home so available, so comfortable.

"Cathy," he asked on one of her frequent visits, "how come a young woman like you who has everything going for her seems so content to be a fifth wheel around us boring old married folks? Aren't you interested in dating at all?"

Cathy's answer was predictable. She didn't find him and his wife boring, she explained. She was so busy during the week, under so much pressure at work and school, she found it relaxing to unwind in such an undemanding, easygoing atmosphere. And besides, she got so caught up with her work, the week seemed somehow just to slip away before she had a chance to make weekend plans. She'd look up from her law books and suddenly it'd be Friday night and she wouldn't have anything to do. And on top of all that, New York was such a cold, unfriendly place.

"Cathy," Jack said, "I want you to know that you're always welcome in this house. Whenever you want to spend time with us just give us a call and drop by. But I think it's unhealthy for you not to be making friends with women your own age or dating men you can start a loving relationship with." And then Jack gave Cathy the one piece of advice that's good for all Office Superstar/Weekend Loners: SET ASIDE WEDNESDAY AS THE DAY TO MAKE PLANS FOR THE WEEKEND.

Jack suggested that on the middle day of the week Cathy spend a few minutes, or an hour, or however long it took, to insure that during the weekend she would have something social to do.

Wednesday is not so early in the week that Cathy would have to spend days in agonizing anticipation of the date she'd planned. But it would give her time to make alternate plans if her original plans fell through. She could call a girlfriend and make plans to go to a dance, make arrangements to play tennis with a male acquaintance, and even find a lecture to attend. The rule was, never let it get past Wednesday without making definite plans for the weekend. Cathy promised she would give it a try.

That next week she called Jack to say that his advice had actually worked. She had called another woman in her law school class and they had decided to find something to go to, like a dance or singles party. Jack and Vivian didn't hear from Cathy for several days. The following week she called to say that she was busy, and that she sent her love but couldn't stop by. In a few months she had an active social life, and was going out regularly. Soon after, she started seeing someone steadily. Today Cathy is in full control of her social life and having a ball. Just that one little trick of reserving Wednesday to make weekend plans did it.

Cathy, besides being shy, had made the common error many people make who are ambitious. She felt that when she became a lawyer, she would then take action to improve her social life. But a lot of office superstars do finally "make it," and still have dull, inactive, social lives. They haven't the vaguest notion of how to change either, because being a weekend loner has become an ingrained habit.

Karen once dated a pleasant, ambitious fellow who had a steady job but was furiously writing the Great American Novel every spare moment. He admitted that when the weekend came along, any inspired writing ended by Saturday night. The words wouldn't flow, and he had no idea what was wrong. Though he longingly envisioned a social life somewhere in the future, perhaps when the novel was completed, he didn't realize how important *now* was. Karen arranged for several weekends of social activity and, as it turned out, the few hours of goofing off and having fun improved his concentration during writing hours immensely.

So, make your plans for the weekend on Wednesday. What you set up doesn't have to be the "date of the century." It can be as simple as a movie with a same-sex friend. This one act will improve your social life immeasurably.

One of the pleasant side benefits of setting up weekend plans in advance is that you can turn back to your work, knowing that when the weekend comes, you'll have something to do. Don't think that Wednesday is too early. It gives people time to get back to you or for you to call someone else. Wednesday leaves nothing to chance. Wednesday is security and confidence. Make plans for the weekend this Wednesday!

20

Be Visible, Go Public

DURING THE worst days of self-consciousness, shy people often hate the way they look. If their hair doesn't fall quite right after their morning shower, it ruins their day. So does a pimple or a few flakes of dandruff or circles under their eyes. And it isn't only physical characteristics that get them feeling dismal about themselves. A bad grade on a paper, an unfulfilling week at the office, saying the wrong thing to a salesperson, or getting tongue-tied and flustered at a meeting—these experiences, too, will leave them feeling unworthy, undesirable, and unlovable. And the more unlovable they feel, the more shyly they behave. After all, how can they approach another human being with any verve or sparkle or energy if they are sure in advance that others aren't going to like them? Most shy people feel defeated before they even get started in their attempts to connect with other people they want to get to know. So defeated, in fact, they often hide at home rather than present—they think—their ugly, hangdog faces to the world. Unless they are having one of their "good-looking days" they won't even go out with the gang after work for a cocktail.

Not-so-shy people, of course, are not nearly so much at the mercy of their internal world, not so reactive to the extreme swings everyone has in the way he or she feels about him or herself. Consequently, the not-so-shy seem more willing to venture forth into the outer world even when things in their inner world aren't coming up roses. They're realistic enough or mature enough or lucky enough to realize that although *they* may be feeling ugly, dull, and lackluster, the world will view them pretty much the way it always views them. Only they themselves have X-ray vision, can see deep down inside, and know what kind of day they are having, a homely or an attractive one, a brave day or a shy day.

The purpose of this chapter is to urge the very shy to begin to behave like the not-so-shy when it comes to being visible and getting out into the world. You can make an effort to be there for others, to go public even on days when you're sure no one, but on one, could possibly be interested in meeting such a loser as you. It's a simple thing to try, really, one that may not pave the way to gracious acceptance by a desirable lovemate, but certainly one that won't open you up to rejection either.

Here's what you have to do. When you're having a bad day, instead of running right home to your room after work or school, find something to do *outside* the house where other people are. If you'd planned on staying home with a good book until that pimple on your chin went away, read at the library instead. If you were going to watch the USC–Notre Dame game on television Saturday afternoon instead of strolling through the park, at least watch it at your neighborhood pub. If you were going to devote the night to your laundry, do it at the local laundromat instead of in your bathroom sink. And *stay* there and read while your laundry is in the washer instead of scampering back to your room. If you were going to eat dinner at home, eat it out. And if it's a weekend and you were going to cook yourself some eggs and bacon for breakfast, let the short-order chef at the corner coffee shop do it for you.

Don't hole up just because you're not feeling up. Only you know how down you are. Ninety percent of the things you do at home you can do publicly in the company of other people. We're not saying you're going to be mobbed by georgos strangers the second you plop yourself down on the bench in front of the Maytag at the laundromat, but certainly you stand an infinitely better chance of meeting someone there than you do in the privacy of your own room.

The point is, life holds more promise for you if you are visible to others, available to others, and approachable. Mary Beth goes to a community college and, to save money, she lives at home with her parents. She's tall and willowy with a striking figure but has a rather plain, often sad-eyed face. Mary Beth is sensitive, quiet, and a brooder. She has few girlfriends and up until six months ago had no boyfriends. Then a curious thing happened. One afternoon Mary Beth stopped off at the library because she needed a reference book for a psychology paper she was writing, intending to spend no more time there than it took her to check out the book. But as luck would have it, one of the professors had the reference work on reserve, and the only way the librarian would let Mary Beth use it was if she sat down and took her notes in the library. Mary Beth was reluctant to do so—her normal routine was to head right home after school and spend the hours between two and five studying in her room—but today she had no choice. So she selected an empty table in the most obscure corner of the library and began her work. A few minutes later someone sat down opposite her. Mary Beth did not look up. She didn't want to see any looks of pity or disappointment as they caught sight of her plain, pale face.

But a few minutes later Mary Beth heard the sound of cellophane being wrinkled. It did not stop, and soon began to interfere with her studying. Mary Beth made up her mind to tell whoever was making the noise to please cut it out. But when she looked up she saw that the boy sitting opposite her already seemed intimidated. He was blushing, and his brow was wrinkled, and he looked nervous and scared. Mary Beth thought she recongized the boy from her French class, one of two awkward, average-looking guys who sat at the very back of the room and whispered a lot.

"Um, excuse me," he managed to get out, all the while fiddling furiously with a pack of Tareytons, "I was going to take a cigarette break. Want to have a smoke with me?" Mary Beth was stunned. This had never happened to her before, a complete stranger asking to spend some time with her. If only I'd set my hair last night, she found herself thinking, or at least had put on a little lipstick in the ladies' room.

"I don't smoke," she said stiffly.

"That's okay," the boy said. "I'll get you a cup of coffee. How about it?"

Too tense to actually say yes, Mary Beth just stood up and followed the boy to the student cafeteria. She felt incapable of opening her mouth, but that was okay because now that she had accepted his invitation the boy seemed quite willing to do all of the talking. Over coffee he confessed that he and his pal from French 101 had decided she, Mary Beth, was the prettiest girl in the class.

The more the boy talked, the more animated and articulate he became. His awkwardness seemed to have disappeared altogether, and Mary Beth couldn't help noticing that up close like this he had very nice warm gray eyes and a lovely smile. When he asked her to go to the movies with him that Friday night, she accepted. Only this time, she thought, I'll be ready for him. And she was.

When the boy rang the doorbell Friday night, he was greeted by a tall stunning young woman with her hair swept back and her face elegantly and immaculately made-up. Mary Beth got a particular bang out of watching his eyes because she could tell he really liked what he saw.

The date was fun but not great. Mary Beth realized that, try as she might, she wasn't all that attracted to the boy. Basically, she still found him average-looking and rather awkward. Still, she was out on a date, and it'd been a long time since she'd been able to say that. She decided even when it's with someone you're not nuts about, a date can be a whole lot more fun than sitting home alone. And that's what led Mary Beth into "going public." It struck her that if she hadn't been in the library earlier in the week, the boy might never have invited her to have coffee with him. It made her realize how much her feelings of being homely and unworthy had been keeping her at home, away from the scrutinizing eyes of her classmates. It made her a little angry with herself. "I suddenly got annoyed that I was letting my fear of what other people might think of me keep me out of the student union, the gym, the library, and all the other places where kids hang out around school. So I decided, hell, girl, you better get yourself looking as good as you can and step out into the world. I started wearing lipstick and dressing better, which made me feel more confident about my appearance, and now I show up everywhere—at basketball games, meetings, you name it. And I'm really starting to meet people. Next weekend I have a date with one boy Friday night and a different one Saturday night, and I can assure you I've never had that to look forward to in my life before."

The moral: If you can do it in public instead of at home, do it. And don't let a pimple or a bad night's sleep or a hole in your sweater send you running back to the privacy of your room. It's as simple as this: You can't meet anyone in your room except maybe your kid brother or your mom or your roommate. To start acting unshy, get out of the house. That mere act will dramatically increase your chances of meeting people to love.

21

Go Out Anyway

THERE'S A great tug-of-war that goes on constantly within the shy person's mind. One side of his or her personality wants to be sociable, outgoing, extroverted. On the other side is the familiar pull to withdraw into narcissistic self-contemplation. For the shy person, the forces in the tug-of-war are never even. The shy aspects of the personality flex their awesome muscles, exert the slightest bit of force, and the battle is lost . . . again. The shy person is defeated, relegated to another night of loneliness and contemplation.

What do you think about when it's time to go out on a weekend? If you're being honest, you find it's thoughts about yourself. Am I dressed right? How should I act? Will I be embarrassed? What if I meet someone and have to talk to him? These thoughts build up, make you terribly self-conscious, and start a neurotic spiral that ultimately prevents you from leaving the house.

On the one hand, you want to go, should go, and need to go. But there's that very persuasive other hand. The one that tells you not to go out in the rain because you'll catch cold. The one that tells you there's a great TV show on that you have to watch. The one that tells you your clothes aren't right for dating.

What should you do in the face of all these powerful negatives? Look at them, recognize them, feel the awful forces pulling at you, feel the gnawing in your stomach and then . . . GO OUT ANYWAY.

Nothing will happen if you stay inside, alone and lonely. You simply have to drag yourself out of the house. It may be difficult, even exhausting, but you *can* do it.

Sara had an awful time going out. She'd come home from work, soak in a hot tub, eat, read for a few hours, and go to bed. She literally spent months in this routine, and when she did have social invitations she would invariably excuse herself by saying her allergies were acting up. Actually, she was shy.

One evening in the spring her college alumni organization held a dance near her home. Several of Sara's sorority sister's had encouraged her to go, and reluctantly she'd agreed.

The weather was balmy the night of the dance, and the spring air was delightfully intoxicating. Thirty minutes before her ride was to pick her up, Sara felt nervous. The tug-of-war began, and she knew she was losing. She began to think how dull her classmates were and what a bore it would be. Desperately, she called her ride to cancel out but it was too late—they had already left. When they pulled up at the door, Sara felt literally nauseous. When a sorority sister appeared at the door, Sara could hardly say hello. Before she could think of an excuse, her friend grabbed her arm and they rushed to the car.

What happened after that sounds like a bit of a fairy tale. There were the usual bland, uninteresting men at the dance. But there was also one very bright, attractive man as well. He approached Sara and, to her surprise, they danced, talked, and later went for coffee. Sara felt her nervousness subside, and although she thought she looked like hell, the man told her she was the prettiest woman at the dance.

Today, Sara laughingly tells that story whenever she and her husband, Bob, visit friends. You guessed it, Bob was the guy Sara met that night at the dance. And all because, despite her fear, panic, and apprehension, she went out anyway.

Former shy people often tell stories about how they have won the war and gotten out the door, even when their minds and bodies wanted to stay home safe and secure.

Harvey, a young man why suffered from severe headaches, got them just at the beginning of the weekend. He went to all kinds of doctors, and they couldn't help him. Finally a wise friend said, "Look, Harvey, why don't you go out anyway? You can't stay home forever and you're not getting better." While this seemed an impossibility to Harvey, he literally dragged himself out with his buddies. At the bar he met a girl and they talked briefly. Although they parted after half an hour, Harvey realized that within five minutes of talking to the girl his headache had vanished. You don't need a psychiatrist to tell you what Harvey's problem was.

You can win your tug-of-war, too. Since no one is going to come to your house, show you toward the door, help you on with your coat and kiss you good-bye, here are a few helpful hints. They'll help you out the door until you no longer need them:

1. A few days before you plan to go out, telephone a few friends or doting relatives and let them know you're going somewhere to meet someone. Make sure you add, "I'll call you and let you know how it went." With your relatives, it's guaranteed they'll call you.

2. Do something exciting to your appearance or buy a new outfit. If you don't go out, you'll feel bad that you went to such trouble and no one will see how special you look. The new appearance may also give you the extra confidence to cross your threshold.

3. Don't have any ready-made excuses. Buy a decent-looking raincoat, hat, umbrella, boots, or whatever else you need to stay warm and dry in foul weather.

4. Make getting wherever you're going as easy as possible. Write the address down. Know how to use public transportation or arrange a ride or take a cab or drive yourself.
5. You don't have to stay! . . . Repeat that and never forget it. Too many shy people feel condemned to boring evenings because they don't know how to leave. If all you can do is stay an hour, okay. But you can't make that decision unless you get there. Besides, you may *want* to stay!

So, short of a 102-degree temperature, a ten-foot blizzard, or a nuclear disaster, no matter how much you want to stay in, go out anyway. Open that door and leave. Do it and you'll win a big battle against your shyness.

No matter how mundane you think a social function will be, if there are other people present who you can meet and talk to, it's worth going. Turn off the TV, close the book, drain the tub, and shut the refrigerator. If you get out over and over again, you'll soon meet someone. And it's the going out anyway that will help get you over your shyness.

22

Something Is Better Than Nothing

WHEN UNSHY people are asked about helping shy people with their problem, they say things like, "It'll be easy to get shy people to improve their social lives. They'll settle for anything." These thoughts are surprising because of how false and unfeeling they are.

The truth is shy people's social expectations often go to the other extreme. Even when they do have dates or relationships, they often view them as inadequate and unsatisfactory. They want prettier girls, handsomer guys, more exciting dates. This is actually a neat and clever device shy people use to help exempt them from challenging social situations. For with the thought of "finding" something better, they often choose to do nothing. This leaves them "comfortably" alone, but also lonely.

Good advice for shy people in this situation is simply: SOMETHING IS BETTER THAN NOTHING. Don't stay home waiting for someone better to suddenly appear at your door. Go out with anyone, whoever it is, whenever you have the chance. Don't punish, attack, or criticize yourself because the person on the other side of the table buttering a breadstick does not resemble Suzanne Sommers or Warren Beatty. It doesn't matter. Going out matters. Do not stop dating someone, or cancel an evening's plans, just to sit home with nothing to do.

Paul, a college senior, never ceased to complain about Claudia, his dull, boring, sexless, unattractive girlfriend. When queried about prolonging his obvious agony, he insisted his shyness prevented him from breaking off with Claudia and dating other women. "At least with Claudia I don't feel self-conscious, and I know she won't reject me."

One miserable evening after dinner and a movie, Paul and Claudia went to a small pub near campus. Paul got up to get drinks at the bar, and as he stood there, a cute cheerleader he had spotted months before accidentally poured her Margarita all over Paul's yellow La Coste shirt. Paul reported that she was so sincerely apologetic and concerned, he wasn't the slightest bit angry. He just smiled and said, "That's all right, this little alligator just loves Margaritas." She laughed, he laughed, and Paul felt a magical moment for the first time in his life . . . and he didn't feel the slightest bit shy.

Paul dated Claudia occasionally after that, but he saw the cute little cheerleader for his entire senior year. He realizes that despite how miserable he was with her, if he hadn't been out with Claudia that particular night he would never have met his athletic cheerleader friend.

This is the point. Every encounter with the opposite sex is a testing ground, an experiment, a practice session for the shy person to master social skills. The "everyday" dates that he or she may not be crazy about are crucial to building confidence for a time when the shy person does have that "special" date.

If you're shy, yet dating someone you're ambivalent about, keep on dating that person anyway, even though you dream in the back of your mind of someone more exciting and attractive.

It's better to practice conversation and the finer points of socializing with someone you frankly couldn't care less about than to plunge headlong into a relationship with someone that makes your heart pound and your eyes spin. While this may sound cold, calculating, and cruel, it's not at all. You don't have to lie or to pledge undying love to the person you are dating. You should just try to date as many people as you can, because for the shy person every opportunity to get out is important.

Something *is* better than nothing. Because nothing is staying home alone and fantasizing about what you want, and something is getting out and fighting your shyness. And who knows, while you're out with someone who doesn't turn you on, you may, like Paul, bump into someone who does. That could never happen if you'd canceled your date and spent the evening in the bathtub.

23

Scare Yourself

ONE OF the most successful tactics to use to act unshy is to: SCARE YOURSELF.

No, you don't have to hide behind a pole and then spring out unexpectedly at our alter-ego yelling "Boo!" at the top of your lungs. Nor do you have to seek out the most terrifying horror movie in town and glue yourself to the screen until you are too terrified to move. You can scare yourself simply by trying to envision what would happen if you kept on saying, "Tomorrow, tomorrow I'll do something about getting a date, about meeting someone, about improving my social life."

You know, there comes a time in every social evening when the shy person faces a crisis, a test of will. It usually happens somewhere between eleven and eleven-thirty, almost when it's too late to take action. What happens is this: Let's imagine for a moment that you're at a party. The crowd is lively, the music is good, the food isn't bad, and there's plenty to drink. Sometime around eleven o'clock the party has hit its prime, it's really cooking. All the guests have arrived, not too many have paired off yet, and everyone's had enough time to knock down a few drinks and get a little bit happy. In short, the evening is in full gear. Now you face your most intense moment of doubt and pain. Up until this time, you have been able to say, "I'm not ready yet, I'm preparing myself, the party hasn't really begun, I don't want to get too tied up with any one person in case someone better happens along." You name it, the excuses abound. But starting around eleven o'clock, the excuses become lame and hollow-sounding, and then you have to admit, "I'm scared. I'm afraid to give the eye to that mysterious-looking man in the blue blazer because I'm afraid he'll turn abruptly away. I'm scared to ask that woman in the Calvin Klein jeans to dance because I'm certain she'll say no." Then what happens is, you just sit there, paralyzed with fear, unable to enter into the fray. You realize that the party or dance will soon begin to peak, that men and women will begin to pair off and head for dark quiet corners, and that those who haven't will get bored and leave for other parties or dances. Yes, the moment has come to spring into action, but you are too scared. And compounding this fear is the realization that the party will soon be on the descendency, that it is going to become increasingly more difficult to meet anyone. This fills you with panic, but still you remain resolute, stolid and unmoving, frozen into inaction.

Half an hour goes by. Now the party is indeed starting to wind down. You think, "Wow, where did everybody go? One minute it's an orgy, the next minute a wake. Oh, well, no use hanging around till the bitter end. Everyone is paired off or gone. There's no one here I'm really interested in. I might as well go home and begin afresh tomorrow. That's what I really need . . . a good night's sleep. Didn't realize how tired I was. Probably couldn't relate to anyone now even if I did meet the love of my life." And so you amble toward the pile of clothes on the bed in the bedroom, find your coat, and head for the door. Sure, you're feeling depressed, but on the other hand, a little bit comfortable, too. Returning home alone is familiar, cozy, comfy. And there's always the thought of a happier, livelier tomorrow to cheer you up. And that thought is the most insidiously dangerous one of all.

Want to know something, shy people? Tomorrow isn't going to be any better than today if you don't do something about it. As you climb into bed alone you can try to comfort yourself all you want that things are somehow automatically going to be brighter, happier, more hopeful in the morning. But unless you make up your mind to be the one who precipitates all this brightness and happiness, chances are life is going to remain pretty much the same. Bleak. Dateless. Without romance.

Want to try a technique that works particularly well during the loneliest, shyest times? Scare yourself. When you're out at a singles bar or a dance or a party, and you sense eleven o'clock is rolling around, don't give in to your inertia, your sleepiness, your impulse to retreat and withdraw inside yourself. Fight. Battle back. Get scared. Think how many times you've given up in the past. Ask yourself how can you possibly expect to take action *next* time when you haven't yet taken action?

People grow more set in their ways—not less. Picture spinster aunts and seedy aging bachelor cousins. Think of all the people who *told* you they were going to write novels . . . and didn't. Or were going to quit their jobs and go out on their own . . . and didn't. Think how easy it is to let the years slip by without doing what you intended to do. History and literature are full of stories of people who let life and romance slip away from them. It happens to millions, you know. And it'll happen to you if you let it, if you don't start doing something about it.

Do you want to meet a dashing professional football player who will take you in his arms and squeeze you until you feel like fainting? Do you want to walk into Studio 54 with a gorgeous actress on your arm? It'll never happen unless you make it happen. Not tomorrow, but tonight, before another wasted evening slips away. Tell that to yourself, shy friends. Tell it to yourself until it scares the living daylights out of you. You can kid yourself all you want that tomorrow, next week, next summer when you've got a tan, next year when you've got your teeth capped, life is going to get better, sexier, more romantic. But the plain, bald truth is that it won't. Things are just going to stay the same unless you take action *now*—TONIGHT!

24

Reaching

REACHING HAS always meant two things to us. First, there's *reaching* as in *reaching beyond yourself*, stretching, seeking, extending. The other definition is closely related yet oddly different, *reaching* in this case meaning arriving, getting there, *reaching your destination*.

What does all this have to do with shyness? To put it bluntly, shy people don't do enough reaching . . . of either kind. In interview after interview, we discovered that shy people almost *never* take chances in the pursuit of love and almost never challenge themselves to do or try something that's the tiniest bit risky, for example, approaching a good-looking guy after class to see if he wants a cup of coffee or walking up to a pretty woman in the park, camera in hand, to snap her picture. Wait a second, that's not quite right. Shy people *do* challenge themselves all the time. In fact, sometimes they set up impossibly difficult quests—

114

get a date with Nick Nolte, ask out Sophia Loren. The only problem is, they rarely *accept* their own challenges.

You might suspect that shy people are probably far less adventurous than the not-so-shy. But you'd be amazed to find out just how universally unadventurous they are. Shy men and women were asked a very simple question: Do you ever take chances? Do you ever walk up to someone in a discotheque, someone to whom you're really attracted, and ask that person to dance? *No. Never. Most of the time we don't ask anyone to dance. And if we do it's only someone who we're sure will accept us, someone who hasn't been asked to dance all evening, someone unattractive or sad-looking, a fellow loser.*

In short, while shy people often aim too high in their fantasy lives, in real life they almost always aim down. If a shy woman considers herself superior to one man, equal to another, and looks up to a third, she will invariably seek out the inferior man instead of her equal or supposed superior. There's less risk, less *reaching*. She's more sure she will be accepted. If for a moment she thinks she'll be rejected, she'll reach even lower. (There's a third definition.) And the same holds true for shy men. The tragedy of all this is that if most people don't do any *reaching* out they stand little chance of *reaching* (arriving at) their full potentials.

Okay, you shy people are probably thinking, *that's true. We don't reach out. We don't take chances. But why rub it in? There's nothing we can do about it. We're simply too shy to reach beyond ourselves. It's too scary.*

Yes, reaching is a little scary. Some shy people are so scared of asking someone to dance, or calling for a date, that they often go six, eight, even twelve months without a single date. And that's awful. They begin to feel so lonely and unloved, it seems like life will never be fun again. And yet slowly but surely things do improve. Not by magic, but by *reaching* out a little at a time, until before long it gets easier and easier to stretch their muscles. And somehow, two or three years later, without quite realizing when the transition has occurred, they think themselves to be strong. They have *reached* their destination.

Harold *reached* beyond himself one day. He took a chance on love, and wound up having the time of his life. Harold is a broker and not a failure by any means, but not particularly successful, either. About ten years ago Harold was living with a woman to whom he wasn't really attracted. "I mean, she was a warm body," he told us, but if he'd had any courage he would have pursued a woman who was funnier, zanier, sexier, prettier. As is typical with shy people, Harold had *reached* down. And because he wasn't happy with the woman, he wasn't happy with himself. And so they fought. Day and night. Weekends were particularly miserable because then they were both home all day and would do nothing but glare across the kitchen table at one another, hating each other and bickering. One gray, humid summer Sunday afternoon, after an argument that nearly became violent, Harold asked the woman to leave. It was in a moment of utter rage and despair, and had he had another minute or two to think about it he would have taken back his words. As much as he had grown to dislike the woman, he was certain that once she was gone he would be alone for the rest of his life. Deep down in his heart he was convinced he was simply too unlovable and unattractive to ever find anyone else. And yet the damage was done. The invitiation to leave had been verbalized, and the woman burst into tears and ran from the apartment. The next day two of her male cousins came in a pick-up truck and cleaned out all her belongings. Who knows, perhaps she too was a shy person living with a man who didn't turn her on and was delighted to be rid of him as well?

The next week for Harold was unbearable. He walked around in a daze—scared, lonely, feeling guilty toward his ex-girlfriend, and afraid for himself. His tiny apartment seemed cavernous, big enough for hordes. One gloomy Wednesday night he sat down with a beer and a copy of *Time* magazine to kill some time. And then suddenly he had an inspiration. *Time* magazine! Why, six months ago a friend had stopped by with a date, Terry, a young researcher at *Time*. She was tall and stately-looking, attractive and worldly. Harold had stared at her all evening long, yearning for her, cursing his shyness, wishing he'd had the courage to *reach* up for a woman like a *Time* researcher rather than down for the woman he was living with. Terry had long black hair and enormous blue eyes. "Maybe I should call her," Harold thought. His friend had moved down to Texas and was no longer dating Terry. And God, how Harold was attracted to her. He fantasized having lunch at a cozy little French restaurant on West Forty-sixth Street, and the image made him dizzy with lust and longing and romance. He resolved to call her the next morning at her office.

That night Harold barely slept. Every time he imagined himself dialing Terry's number, a shot of adrenalin would slice through his stomach, making him writhe and twist in his bed.

That morning Harold sat at his desk trying to concentrate on his stock listings, but the phone on his desk kept beckoning him, tempting him. "Don't call her, you fool," he cautioned himself. "Don't be an idiot. She'd never accept a date with the likes of you. You're too homely for her, not exciting or rich or glamorous enough. She's too pretty, too intelligent. Leave her alone." But still the thought arose in his mind. What if she accepts? What if for some crazy absurd reason she'd been attracted to him, too, the night they'd first met?

Suddenly Harold found himself reaching for the phone. His face felt chilly, his mind numb, his consciousness dim and receding. He stuck his finger in the dial and reeled off the seven numbers. . . . Before he knew it an operator was intoning, "Can I help you?"

"I'd like to speak to Terry Raylanz," Harold heard himself say. A moment later a pleasant, upbeat voice was answering, "Terry Raylanz." Harold hemmed and hawed and reintroduced himself. "Oh, sure, I remember you," said the woman. "How's Susan?"

"We broke up," Harold replied.

"Oh, that's too bad. I'm sorry."

"Don't be. It was the best thing. We'd started hating each other. Listen, would you like to have lunch today?" Somehow the words had burst out of Harold's mouth like the flock of six-and-twenty blackbirds out of the king's pie, as if they'd had a life of their own. Harold sat glumly waiting for the refusal. Oh, well, at least he'd asked. It was the bravest thing he'd ever done in his life.

"Sure," the pretty researcher answered. "But I can't go until after one o'clock. We go to press today. Is that okay?"

"Yeah, sure," Harold mumbled. He was so thoroughly stunned he almost forgot to tell her the name of the restaurant they'd be lunching in.

When he hung up the phone, he leapt out of his chair and literally danced around his office. What luck! What fantastic, incredible, wonderful luck! He'd just done the wildest, most spontaneous, boldest thing in his life, and for some reason—he would never understand why—the woman had answered yes. He simply couldn't believe it.

Lunch turned out to be great. Terry, feeling the afterglow magazine people feel when they've finally put an issue to bed, indulged herself in a second and a third glass of wine. As Harold walked her back to her office, she took his arm and leaned her head on his shoulder for a moment. She mentioned something about having a very stuffy party to go to Sunday night and would he mind terribly being her escort. She knew it wouldn't be much fun at the party, but maybe they could go out for a few drinks afterward. Again Harold felt as if he were being followed around by some kindly, invisible fairy godmother.

The Sunday-night party was dull, but Harold was so happy to be with Terry he didn't care. Afterward they did go out for drinks as planned, and both got a little bit tipsy. When Harold walked her to her apartment door, Terry invited him in. Within an hour they were making love in her narrow but adequate bed. Harold, of course, was in a state of euphoria, the conquering hero heady with success. The next morning, perhaps for the first time in his life, he rode the bus to work feeling like a regular member of the human race instead of his shy, unworthy, *different* old self.

Terry and Harold dated constantly over the next month, and the really odd thing is that after about three weeks Harold grew bored with her. She no longer seemed as pretty and sexy as he'd remembered. Her legs were heavy, he noticed, and her chin protruded, and she droned on and on about *Time* as if it were the most significant piece of journalism being written in the world today. The relationship ended finally when Harold simply stopped calling for dates.

But that was hardly the end of Harold's newfound social expertise. The experience of having done something so seemingly rash and dangerous and risky—and having survived—emboldened him. He asked out a receptionist in his firm, a young woman from Liverpool whom nearly every broker in the place coveted. She was busy. Rather than feeling hurt and put down, Harold found himself annoyed. How could she? She didn't know what she was missing. He instantly rushed back to his office and called a woman he'd met the other day in his apartment building. When he proposed a movie for that evening, she responded with downright enthusiasm.

Well, you needn't worry about Harold anymore. His one act of *reaching* helped him *reach* his potential as a social being. Almost overnight. Can you do the same? Perhaps. It is difficult for shy people to go beyond themselves, to stretch their social muscles. It can be the most terrifying notion of all, scarier than the thought of radioactive fallout, earthquakes, tornadoes. But for the first time, think about it. Entertain the idea of *reaching* out, striving, taking chances. Imagine yourself asking that devilishly handsome account executive in the next office if he'd like the extra ballet ticket your sick friend can't use. Play with the idea of seeing if your beautiful new neighbor wants to stop by at the bar around the corner for a fast beer. Sometimes just fantasizing an action can lead you to it. It certainly can't hurt, that is, unless fantasizing becomes the focal point of your existence. Who knows, one day soon maybe the mere fact that you've been contemplating *reaching* beyond yourself will carry you over the edge and you'll do it.

25

Using the Telephone

IN YOUR home right now is a tool that, if used properly, can activate your social life with amazing suddenness and success: The Phone.

Some people don't feel comfortable on the phone; it makes them nervous, and voices on the other end of the line seem overly powerful and intimidating. But others like it, saying that the phone gives them a feeling of confidence and ease they don't have in face-to-face confrontation. In fact, many people who now have active social lives would never have had the courage to ask for a date or make plans with friends for a social function if it hadn't been for the phone.

Consider what the phone allows you to do. By simply picking up the receiver and dialing a seven-digit number you can call three, four, five, even ten people in the time it would take you to visit one. The phone enables you to talk to people without spending hours grooming and beautifying, only to have a strained conversation with a stranger in a crowded singles bar. No, you don't have to get dressed, you don't have to look good, you don't even have to feel good. The only thing you need in order to have a wonderful conversation with someone on the phone is the ability to open your mouth and talk. Don't take that marvelous invention of modern technology for granted—the phone is a potent weapon in your battle against shyness.

Fred is the perfect example of someone who discovered the latent power of the phone. For three years he had a job selling advertising space over the phone for a mid-western newspaper. Although unbelievably shy when meeting women face-to-face, Fred had developed an effective, assertive, likable telephone manner that won him several new accounts every month. He spoke as easily with the presidents of corporations as he did with employees from a nearby delicatessen—men and women alike.

One afternoon, after Fred had mentioned to a co-worker that once again he didn't have a date for the weekend, the man suggested Fred use his vast telephone contacts for social as well as business purposes. The suggestion seemed immediately exciting and revelatory to Fred.

That very afternoon he began to spend two or three minutes of every phone conversation with female clients discussing the small talk of the day. After a week he discovered that Susan Johnson from the dress warehouse two towns over was single and a tennis fanatic. Over the next month Fred not only set up a weekly tennis date with Susan, but he went to five lunches, three dinners, the theater, and a baseball game, entered two bike races, and spent a weekend at the beach, all with other attractive, eligible young women who had been only business acquaintances previously. For Fred, the phone truly is a blessing that has altered his life.

In this chapter, you are going to find out how to call someone you'd like to go out with and make a date with that person. No, this is not an exercise directed only to men. Women can do exactly the same thing. There's a sherry commercial on the air now in which a woman phones a man to ask him over for an after-dinner drink. You can be sure that if a giant marketer feels it's now safe to portray this on television, it's been going on all over the place for years.

Several years ago, one of the authors wrote a book called *How to Ask a Man*, and in it she explored the various ways women could assert themselves and approach men without turning themselves inside-out or turning the men off. As part of her research she interviewed scores of men to probe their feelings about being telephoned by women for dates. The unanimous response was, "I'd love a woman to call me once in a while. I'd feel so flattered." Women can ask a man to come to dinner, for example, or to a small party.

Of course, when it comes to the telephone, shy people already have a modus operandi. And that is to *wait* for the phone to ring. It does, sometimes, and the voice on the other end proposes something you'd like to do. But how often does that happen? Once or twice a year? On the other hand, if you pick up the phone *before* it rings and do the dialing yourself, you can make something happen every day of the year.

Choose, right now, someone you've met somewhere—at a party or at work or wherever. This should be a person within your reach, not someone you're fantasizing about who's living with someone or doesn't know you exist. It should be someone you're attracted to, someone you'd like to spend some time with and get to know better. Step-by-step, here is all you have to do:

1. *Prepare a positive introduction.* It can be witty, straightforward, usual or unusual. It doesn't matter. Ten minutes later the person you are asking out won't even remember what you said initially. You might want to write down your introduction as a prop to get you off and running, so you don't lose your nerve or become tongue-tied or get off the beaten track. It could be as simple as this minispeech: "Hi, Ralph, this is Karen. We met at Marsha's party. My roommate can't use her ticket to the Willie Nelson concert next week and I suddenly remembered you said you loved country music. . . ."

Then put aside your speech and state your suggestion, which obviously is that Ralph put your roommate's ticket to good use by accompanying you to the Willie Nelson concert or tennis match or Bergman film or whatever. If Ralph is a person you've met but don't yet know very well, pick an event built around a common interest.

2. *Body of Conversation.* This is, believe it or not, the least important part of your conversation and it occurs after you've asked the person for a date. It might be a long, satisfying chat or a short one. If the person is unable to accept your invitation, there's no need to hang up immediately. Feel the person out first to see whether other arrangements can be made. Remember, if you begin to feel uncomfortable or clam up on the phone, all you have to do is say you're late for a date and hang up.

3. *Closing.* Confirm the date in your closing. Fix the exact date, time, meeting place, and say, "I'm looking forward to seeing you." If the answer has been a no, don't act like you've been rejected. Say very calmly and cooly, "Perhaps some other time."

Here is a sample conversation consisting of How Not to Call (for men) and How to Call (for women):

THE WRONG WAY TO CALL

"Hi, Nan, this is Ed."
"Hi." (*Ed who?*)
"So, what's new?"
"Nothing much."
"Oh, well, what did you think of the election results?"
"I'm not into politics myself."
"Oh. Say, I was wondering if . . ."
"Excuse me, there's someone at the door."

(pause)

"Listen, I have to go now. I have company."
"Oh, sure. Nice talking to you."

THE RIGHT WAY TO CALL

"Hi, Ed, this is Sue Smith."

"Oh, hi."

"Say, I really enjoyed talking to you at Marsha's party last night about Blue Grass music and I had a great idea . . ."

"Yeah?"

"There's a concert on Tuesday and it just so happens my roommate can't use her ticket. So I have an extra. Would you like to go?"

"Sure."

"Well, why don't you pick me up at my place at seven-thirty."

"Okay, swell. Say, what's the program? I read about that concert."

(brief chat)

"Well, Ed, I have to run. My laundry's downstairs in the dryer. I'm really looking forward to seeing you next Tuesday at seven-thirty. Oh, by the way, sometimes my buzzer sticks so ring a few times so I can hear it."

(Note: In the first sample conversation, Ed had a sloppy introduction. He never got to the point, didn't assume Nan might be busy, and when she said she had to go, neglected to tell her he'd call her at a more convenient time. In the second sample conversation, Sue gets right to the point. Also, she never mentions that she bought two tickets with the hope of finding a male companion. Only that she has them. She adroitly turned the invitation into a date by asking Ed to pick her up at her home.)

According to the law of averages, there is a certain ratio of success that will be yours if you call enough people. Salespeole know this. People who look for a job are aware of it. The simple act of consistent, methodical phoning will sooner or later begin to bring you more people to date than you could have ever imagined. The more you phone, the better you get at it, and the more comfortable and confident you feel.

Here's something that might work for you. Give yourself a goal to call a certain number of people weekly to ask out or in for a date. One very shy guy did this, committing himself to calling two girls a week come rain or come shine. Two years ago he hardly went out at all. Now he always has someone to go out with because he knows how to use the telephone.

Decide how many phone calls you want to make a week and stick to it. One phone call is acceptable, but, remember, the more people you call the more people you'll soon be able to add to your list of *datables.*

To phone people for dates is *unshy* behavior. After all, shy people just don't do that much of it. The reason phoning is so useful to shy people is that it's the kind of outgoing behavior that's easy to do. You don't need to smile, act friendly, or look anyone in the eye. You don't have to stand up tall, keep from blushing, or even keep your composure. When you phone, you're usually all by yourself and can blink, turn red, slouch, pull your hair, grimace, and, in the event of panic, simply say, "Excuse me, I've got to run," and hang up.

In short, you have everything to gain and nothing to lose and your preparations can be as inexpensive, easy, and quick as the time it takes to follow the aforementioned instructions.

So, the next time you get your phone bill, there should be a slight increase. That will show you're using your phone to call more people. Every extra penny is well worth it. In fact, if the disco around the corner has a five-dollar cover charge and you just tend to hang around for an hour and split anyway, take one evening and use that five dollars for your phone calls. Sit down in the comfort of your own home and dial yourself a date.

Think of it this way. If you're shy and lonely, you may feel the journey to a busy, fulfilling social life is difficult and long, that it'll be months, perhaps even a year, until you've found someone to love. Yet if you have a telephone at hand you could end your loneliness with as simple an action as dialing seven numbers with your forefinger and muttering a few sentences. That one act could solve your shyness problem in one fell swoop for the rest of your life—without you ever having to dress up, look your best, dance, buy drinks, or even leave your bed. That's how powerful a tool the telephone can be.

After all, one phone call to get a date could lead to *that* date. That date could lead to a relationship. The relationship could lead to an engagement. The engagement most usually leads to marriage—and there you are. All because of one phone call!

26

Positive Projection

IT'S ASTONISHING how competent an image even the shyest people can project when they're doing something at which they're skilled or talented. One retiring young woman is an excellent flutist. At a cocktail party she cowers in the corner. Yet at a recital she sits up tall and proud, her face alive with fiery concentration, her body swaying freely and sensuously to the music. It is curious, this enormous twain in the shy person's personality. What would happen if shy women or men could bring to a social encounter the same sense of self, of positive projection, that they display when they're doing something which they enjoy, which is comfortable for them.

This idea was proposed to one of the young researchers who has helped so much in putting together this book. His name is Chuck, and as competent and sure of himself as he is at work, he is awkward and shy around attractive, single women of his own age. "Chuck," he was asked, "what would happen if you could be as forward and as confident at parties and singles bars as you are at your job?"

"Why, I'd have all the dates I wanted," he replied. "But I'm not. Around women I'm attracted to, I get flustered. I mumble and stare at my feet, and unless they really seem to like me and let me know it in no uncertain terms, I usually just fade into the woodwork."

"Well, what if the next time you met a woman you liked, you pretended that getting to know her was part of your job? Suppose you thought of her as a doctor you wanted to interview, or a librarian you were trying to talk into tracking down an obscure book?" Chuck was asked.

Chuck's curiosity seemed piqued. He was well-aware of the theory that the fastest, most effective way to conquer shyness is simply to act unshy. He wasn't totally certain he could pull it off, but he agreed to give it a try. A few nights later Chuck visited a local singles bar with several of his friends; it was a place where college students and young professionals congregate during summer vacation.

He walked up to the bar standing straight and tall. Quite near him he was aware of an attractive young woman who was having trouble hailing the bartender. Chuck said to her, "Tell you what. I'll get the bartender for you. Doesn't mean I'm going to buy you the drink, but I'll get his attention so you can order."

She said, "Well, thanks, that's kind of you."

Chuck spoke up in a strong, positive voice much like the one he uses on the telephone around the office. "Bartender, this young lady would like a drink." The bartender came her way immediately and she got her drink. Then she and Chuck began to chat.

They tossed off the usual lines. "Come here often?" "Are you from around here?" and after two or three minutes of small talk, the young man fixed the girl with his eyes and said, "I want to go out with you Tuesday night. I think we'll have a great time."

The girl stared at him. Then she said, "Okay, fine." And she gave him her telephone number. Only his exterior was positive. On the inside he was shaking and feeling negative and thoroughly inadequate.

When they went out on the date, the woman admitted, "You know, I *never* go out with a man I meet in a singles bar until we've had lunch or I have seen him there a few times at least. But you were so sure of yourself, so positive, I somehow immediately trusted you. There was no room for me to say no. Afterward, I asked myself why I said yes that fast. I guess that's why."

Next time you head out for a night on the town, give Positive Projection a try yourself. Think of an area in which you're particularly skilled or comfortable. Maybe you have great confidence on the softball field, at ballet class, or briefing a jury. Then, see if you can isolate in your mind the stance, the tone of voice, the facial demeanor that is yours when you're doing "your thing." The next step, of course, is to try to project the *softball you*, the *ballet you*, the *lawyer you* at a party or a singles bar. This is the "you" that's a winner, and if you can succeed in bringing that you along to your next social event, you may very well be a winner there, too.

RULES FOR POSITIVE PROJECTION

1. *Good Posture*—Stand up straight. Sit up straight. Carry yourself well.
2. *Positive Voice*—If you're not hunched over, you won't be talking into your chest and you will sound more positive right away. Make sure your voice is loud enough to be heard. Watch that the modulation is low and pleasing. Speak clearly and slowly. Don't crowd your conversation with unnecessary words. Say just what you need to say to get your point across.
3. *Direct Eye Contact*—Look at the person in the eye.
4. *Smile*—And do it often.

5. *Give Off Good Vibes*—Actually, if you follow Numbers 1
    to 4, most likely you will be doing this automatically. Try
    to keep in mind that you are special. Worth meeting.
    Even if deep down inside you think you're not.

If you do all this, you will be trying what Chuck did that night
at the singles bar. Even if you feel you're boring or ugly or you've
got pimples and nobody's going to like you, just try being Mr. or
Ms. Positive. You have no idea how easy it is to sweep people
into your special aura.

Many of the people you meet at parties or dances or bars or
discos feel in their innards the same way you do at times—
inadequate, insecure, and uncomfortable. And when they meet
someone positive, as you are pretending to be, they are attracted
to you as a butterfly is to a flower. It's as simple and as easy as
that.

Here is a caution on the don'ts. DO NOT:

1. Stand like you're going to give a military salute. That's
    too straight. That's rigid, not positive.
2. Put the *wrong* kind of authority in your voice or so much
    authority you become overbearing. That will scare people
    away.
3. Glare at the person under arched eyebrows. Make sure
    your face is relaxed. Tension is the culprit and you'll have
    to constantly remind your face to soften.
4. Flash a smile that's a sneer. Again, you may not know
    you're doing this. It's nerves. Keep it in mind.
5. Give off Pompous Vibes. This is when everything
    backfires. People won't think you're shy or positive.
    They'll think you're a little stuck on yourself.

Remember, this is an action—not an analytical—book. The
fastest and happiest way to a better social life is through a
confident and self-assured appearance. Millions upon millions

of people are jelly inside. It is those who have most successfully mastered the art of projecting an engaging, unafraid personality who seem to have an easier time making dates and finding love. Try Positive Projection soon. You'll be amazed at how successful you'll be.

27

Learning the Art of Small Talk

MANY SHY people just disdain small talk. While others unself-consciously open conversations with comments about the weather, shy people remain silent because they fear being boring, unoriginal. They are sure that if they ever looked up from the gory pictures in their morning newspaper to say to a neighboring straphanger, "God, what a terrible plane accident," he or she would snort contemptuously and move to another subway car. They are very wrong!

As your desire to free yourself from the shackles of shyness intensifies, begin to study how others open conversations with strangers. You'll notice how often people use opening lines that sound inane, clichéd, and trite. In movies and books, heroes and heroines exchange clever, witty remarks. In real life, the opposite seems to be the rule. "Hot enough for yous" abound, while scintillating conversation is rare and often goes unappreciated.

The fact is, most people seem to prefer small talk. They enjoy conversing about the weather, who won the academy awards, how the new cars all look alike this year. Small talk helps to unleash the thoughts that are on the tip of everyone's tongue. To be sure, even the most ordinary citizens have profound inner reflections on death, humor, love, sex, and religion buried in the deep recesses of their mind. But, for whatever reason, the great majority of the people you come across in this world would rather leave their complex thoughts where they are, particularly when first getting to know a stranger.

Granted, small talk can appear boring, unchallenging, and even hypnotizing in its dullness. It sometimes feels like sawdust in your mouth. But once you discover its immense power to interest your fellow women and men, to make them feel good, to help them to trust and like you, you can begin to employ it whenever you see someone you are drawn to. "Nice day," you'll say with a smile to the attractive person standing next to you on the elevator, "That looks good," to someone about to dig into a cheeseburger at the luncheonette around the corner. The results will be everything you are hoping for and often more. The stranger will usually smile and come back with a comment equally as pedestrian. And you in return can feed them another piece of small talk until pretty soon the two of you are involved in a full-scale conversation. From there it's easy to continue on to topics more profound and fulfilling. But there's nothing like small talk to get things off the ground. If you're not convinced, just spend the next few weeks eavesdropping on the people around you. You'll be astonished at the frequency with which small talk is used in office reception areas, at lunch counters, in pubs, on commuter trains and buses. And you'll be even more astonished at its acceptance.

During a bus ride one morning, two strangers were overheard striking up a conversation. One asked directions, adding that he had just moved in from out of town. "Oh, yeah?" the woman replied, "Where are you from?" Then followed a whole conversation about the transportation system, how difficult it is to learn, and where you could make mistakes. When the bus reached the central terminal, the man cheerfully said, "Thanks for a pleasant conversation. How about if I repay you with a cup of coffee?"

"Love to," said the woman and they strolled off, chatting away, toward the nearest McDonalds. So don't torture yourself trying to be Shakespeare. It's not necessary. Don't clam up because you're convinced nothing you can think up could possibly impress anyone. People don't want to be impressed. They want to be liked, listened to, and appreciated. Just keep your ear open for small talk. And practice using it yourself whenever you get the chance.

Included here is a list of several pieces of small talk to help get you started. All of them can get you into a conversation with just about anyone you want. Co-workers, classmates, neighbors, receptionists—anybody you'd like to talk to. Read them and give them a try. You'll be amazed at what trusty icebreakers they are. At first glance, they might seem terribly pedestrian, but it's amazing the way they work:

- What do you think of this weather we've been having?
- *(To someone reading a popular novel)* Hey, I hear that's terrific.
- Seventy-five cents for a cup of coffee. Talk about inflation!
- What a cute dog! What kind is it?
- I think it looks like rain.
- *(Stepping off an elevator)* If I'd known we were going to stop at every floor, I would have taken the stairs.
- *(To someone buying any new and heavily advertised product, at a supermarket, for example)* Is it any good?
- *(The day after an election)* Four years of so-and-so to look forward to.

Small talk works a little like a Ping-Pong game. You serve your opener. The other person relates an anecdote or tells a story while you listen. Then it's your turn again. There's no need to be brilliant or personal or deep. Just play the game of friendly small talk. Even if you would rather be discussing the symbolism in T. S. Eliot's poetry, you'll find small talk a magnificently powerful way to meet new people.

28

Silence Can Be Golden

MANY SHY people have mentioned that when they're introduced to someone at a party or a dance, they often have trouble thinking of something to say. When among friends, they report, conversation seems to come easily. When they're with strangers their minds suddenly seem void of interesting ideas.

This can be a problem, of course, but it's not nearly as serious as you think. You see, while you may fear the silences that inevitably pop up in a conversation, your companion may hardly notice them. The fact is silence is as much a part of the natural cadence of conversation as words themselves. Listen in on a couple sitting next to you in a restaurant. During the course of the meal they'll probably spend far less than half the time in actual conversation. The only difference is that while you'd be in agony during the silences, they're quite content to gaze at each other or the other diners.

You should be aware of the *naturalness* of silence because shy people often leap to fill a void in a conversation even when they have nothing important or interesting to say. Sometimes they blurt out something perfectly inappropriate—their phobic fear of wolves, their penchant for weeping, or their inability to sleep without hugging their pillow. But you should know that it is no more your responsibility to fill a silence than your companion's. And while you may find the silence a grim, thundering reminder of your shyness, your date is probably not even remotely aware of it. Or if he is aware of it, his need to fill the silence may be even more urgent than your own.

Some shy people are so panicked by the sound of silence that they will fill it with anything—usually with something overly personal or boring beyond words. The result is that instead of using silence to regain their composure, to take a deep breath and relax, they turn off their date by revealing too much too soon, or by putting them to sleep with dull, nervous chatter.

If you're one of these shy people who overracts in your efforts to drown out a silence, stop! It isn't easy, but if you're resolute you can do it. You've probably seen too many dates look at you peculiarly out of the corner of their eye as you droned on about the terrible acne you suffered through in your sophomore year of high school or your unusual but brilliant analysis of *Beowulf*. So put yourself on a word budget. It is certainly better than blabbing your guts out the instant your companion stops talking.

You will discover that silence can indeed be golden. One simple decision to say less rather than more will lead to an immediate and marked improvement in your social life. When in doubt, shut your mouth. When there is silence, wait for your date to break it. Sometimes you may almost go mad biting your tongue. You may feel that the fact that your date isn't talking is a sign that she hates you . . . or at the very least she is bored by you. But difficult as it is, persevere. In so doing you will stop turning off, and in some cases start turning on, a would-be lover. And rest assured, a real lover is much more romantic and fun than a would-be one.

Now, of course, this isn't to say that it's advisable to be silent all the time. That's just as harmful, maybe even more so, than talking too much. Don't use this chapter as an excuse to give into a natural predilection to clam up altogether. But, if a silence arises, that's okay. Don't panic. Don't become depressed. It doesn't mean your date doesn't like you. And it doesn't mean you have to jump right in and get the dialogue going again. Silence is a natural part of the rhythm of conversation, of life, and when it occurs it's not a glaring indicator of your shyness. Use it to rest. Use it to relax. Use it to look at your date and communicate how you feel about him or her with your eyes, your smile, and your bearing.

In the next chapter you'll learn how to be a good listener. This is just as important as being a good talker . . . and is another important tool for people who are shy to master when they don't feel they have anything to say.

29

The Power of Positive Listening

No, THIS is not like one of those articles that tell you the way to find romance is to shut your mouth and bat your eyes as some crashing bore bends your ear all evening about his or her third cousin's best friend's romance with Bruce Springsteen. We know you've already read about the value of being a good listener.

The recent rash of How to Be a Good Listener articles that seem to be popping up in every self-help book and magazine really are a putoff. The advice that's being served up somehow seems so wimpish: Look at your date adoringly, flare your nostrils as a sign of interest, and listen in silence for the next five hours as whoever is sitting on the other side of the table from you drones on about his (usually this advice is aimed at women) job selling computers for IBM. How boring! What a sad suppression of one's own personality and ego! And for what? To butter up some inconsiderate boor in the hope that if you're worshipful enough he may take a liking to you? Forget it.

Yet here you are given the same advice. The only difference is the rationale in this book. You don't have to polish your listening skills primarily to get people to like you. That's just a side benefit. The real reason you should open your mind to the power of positive listening is because it gives you a chance to tread water when you can't think of anything to say—and when you're about to panic because you feel yourself clamming up.

Why, the ability to listen well is one of the shy person's greatest fallback positions. You can put it to good use whenever you find yourself beginning to babble on inanely out of nervousness. You simply ask your date a question and then sit back and listen as you work at calming yourself down, or at finding your social equilibrium. The fact that your interested face might be charming your companion is just a happy coincidence. What you are really focusing on is relaxing and getting over your momentary panic. Of course, while you are going about the business of relaxing you can't stare dumbly at your companion with crazed, unseeing eyes. He or she will immediately sense that you really aren't listening at all. At the very least you have to give your date the impression that you're taking in everything that's being said. And that's why it's so important to know how to listen well.

How can you master this skill?

Your school is right in your home. Your television set. Tune in Merv Griffin, Johnny Carson, Dick Cavett, and Dinah Shore. And watch how they listen. You'll discover that these talk show hosts are geniuses at listening with their eyes, their ears, and their whole bodies. A guest may be blabbering away about his trained pet giraffe or her bottle-cap collection that's worth a million dollars. But whether the guest is discussing a fascinating subject or telling the most boring story of the last ten years, he always gets the talk show host's undivided attention. One would think the guest had climbed to the mountaintop and brought back the ten commandments, so rapt and attentive is the listener.

Several years ago one of the co-authors of this book was a

guest on the Merv Griffin show. Now this wasn't the first talk show he'd ever done. He'd stayed up until five in the morning once answering call-ins on the Joe Podunk radio show. And he'd traveled to Baltimore one morning to appear live on the Brenda Fenda Hour, along with a woman who was an expert on shooing aphids off tomato plants. But Merv Griffin was the Big Time, national TV, with a panel of famous, glamorous guests. To put it mildly, the author was scared to death. To this day he still has no recollection of how he managed the 100-foot walk from the wings to the chair at Merv's side. All he remembers for sure is some stagehand giving him a good hearty shove, and next thing he knew he was looking out at an enormous audience of curious, demanding faces. Boy, was he nervous! And that's when he noticed Merv. He was staring at the author eagerly with gigantic, sympathetic eyes. His expression was warm, friendly, accepting. He looked at the author as if he just couldn't wait to hear what he had to say. And did that ever help! Suddenly he didn't feel nervous anymore. Merv asked a question, and before the author got out his first sentence, Merv was devouring the answer with his ears, his eyes, his entire being. He just couldn't seem to get enough of what the author had to say. Now this author is not so naive as to think that Merv really found what he had to say all that interesting. After all, here's a man who's interviewed Orson Welles, Tallulah Bankhead, and Truman Capote. But for those fifteen minutes or so that the author was out on stage, Merv sure made him feel interesting, profound, important. And he'll never forget Merv for it.

You can learn a lesson from Merv Griffin and the other great talk show hosts. They know how to listen, to bring a guest alive with their ability to make him or her feel vital, important, fascinating. And you can do the same—at a party, on a date, in a discotheque or a singles bar. You can make your companion feel brilliant, funny, wise, and original simply by learning how to listen well. And the wonderful thing is that while all this is going on you'll quietly and privately be getting your unshy act together.

In addition to watching talk show hosts, you ought to learn the listening skill that psychologists call echoing. The following sample conversation will show you how it works:

TALKER: "So then I looked down and found the earring on the ground."
LISTENER: "On the ground?"
TALKER: "Uh-huh. I thought it was lost and it was right there in the bushes and I found it one week later!"
LISTENER: "One week later! Wow!"

Here's another way to listen passively without actually repeating your companion's words.

TALKER: "I dunno. There aren't many places to meet people around here. Last night I went to this disco . . ."
LISTENER: "Uh-huh . . ."
TALKER: "And I saw this really terrific-looking woman. I mean she was a knock-out."
LISTENER: "Yeah."
TALKER: "So I asked her if she wanted to dance and the funniest thing is, after she opened her mouth, I just didn't find her all that attractive."
LISTENER: "No kidding?"

You'll be delighted at how easy it is to launch right into echoing the moment you feel yourself beginning to clam up. So, next time you're chatting with someone at a party or on a date, and suddenly your old familiar feelings of unworthiness and unattractiveness rise up to suffocate you, don't panic, don't flee, don't excuse yourself and disappear into the john for half an hour. Simply ask a question to get your companion started on a story or anecdote. And then, as she talks on, punctuate her comments with your echoing skills. You'll find this technique will give you more than enough time and breathing space to calm yourself down. And who knows, because you've become such a good listener, maybe your companion will have fallen head over heels in love with you by the time you're ready to begin speaking again.

30

What to Do When You Clam Up

TWO IDEAS were introduced in the preceding chapters that you could put to work whenever you found yourself having difficulty conversing. One was to sit back and enjoy the silence until you could think of something appropriate to say. And two was to use your listening skills to coax your companion to fill the silence until you felt ready once again to participate yourself.

In this chapter you'll discover what you can do if, one, you simply can't get used to the sound of silence and, two, no amount of brilliant listening on your part succeeds in getting your date to speak up. It can happen. And five minutes of silence while watching a traffic light change, pushing string beans across your plate, or shifting from one foot to another at a party is admittedly no picnic. In a situation like that even a relatively self-assured person can begin to panic.

To help keep *you* from panicking, here are three techniques you can employ during your shyest, most self-effacing days. Give any or all of them a try the next time the cat's got your date's tongue as well as your own. You'll find that with the help of the following antishyness exercises, instead of fleeing for home or falling into a depression for the rest of the evening, your spirits will begin to revive, your self-confidence will soar, and your chances of having a good time will increase vastly.

1. *Search for your anger.* Instead of automatically blaming yourself for the eerie silence that is taking place as you drive to the cinema or stroll through the park, explore the notion of blaming it on your companion. After all, your companion is being just as quiet as you are. And if she would just say something, *anything*, you'd be only too glad to take her up on it. When you think about it, it's just not fair that she clammed up like this. Here you've spent hours getting ready for this date, washed your hair, put on your best clothes, and Dummy on the opposite side of the table is sitting there like a sphinx. Why don't people ever stop playing these stupid, childish games of intimidation?

Get the picture? The silence that is taking place is probably even less your fault than your companion's. And if you can get really angry about it, you'll begin to stop panicking and start coming back to life, to the present. You may even get up the nerve to say something like, "Hey, are you still alive over there?"

2. *Find your sexuality.* Nick, a young copywriter, once went out to dinner with a date to whom he was maddeningly physically attracted. For months he had been having the most vivid sexual fantasies about this person. And now he was going out with her.

As you might expect, he was more than a little bit nervous. So much so, in fact, that when the waiter placed his favorite dish, sautéed softshell crabs, down in front of him, he could barely take a mouthful. His date was busily ingesting steak *au poivre*, concentrating mightily on each bite, and all Nick could think about was how ugly he looked with food in his mouth, how things weren't working out as he'd dreamed, how his date was being unusually quiet, and how sad it was that his hair hadn't parted the way he'd wanted. Panic began to set in. The evening was now more than half over, and he'd gotten nowhere in terms of warming up his date. The conversation so far had seemed wooden and formal. His date appeared more interested in the food than him. And he was sure it wasn't his imagination that some sort of flirtation was going on between his companion and a diner several tables in back of him. A deep, morbid depression began to settle over him, and he thrashed about madly in the recesses of his mind to find a trick, an idea, a gimmick to break the pattern of escalating self-doubt. Nick had goofed up too many relationships in the past. He was out with a prized person tonight, and he wanted to make the most of it. And here is the technique he came up with.

He'd noticed that during the entire meal he'd felt absolutely sexless. Normally, a mere glimpse of his date from a distance of several hundred paces was enough to start his heart pounding. Yet tonight, with her warm body not twenty-four inches away, Nick felt nothing. He began to concentrate on feeling some of his lost sexual impulses. He looked at his date's thick, luxuriant hair, her tongue as she opened her mouth to take a bite of steak, her wide, clear eyes, and her slim firm body. He took a deep breath trying to capture her aroma, her aura. He imagined what it would be like to be stranded on a desert island with her, the two sole survivors of a shipwreck. Even if she doesn't find me attractive, he gloated, in a week or two she'd be feverish to make love to me. All this thinking had its desired effect. Slowly but surely he soon began to once again feel an intense physical attraction for the person sitting opposite him. And in a subtle but nevertheless noticeable way this helped to revive his flagging spirits, added a degree of color to his cheeks, and put a sparkle in his eye. Even more importantly, it made him feel more energetic, more charged up. Try this technique yourself and see if it doesn't bring your whole persona back to life.

3. *Find a temporary retreat.* Sometimes, to get over a

"silence panic" you literally have to leave the room. So go ahead and do it. Walk away and treat yourself to a "Tension Break." The very act of moving around makes the blood in the brain circulate faster and will give you more energy, make you feel less like a sleepwalker.

If you're at a dance or disco or party or restaurant or whatever, just excuse yourself and go to the rest room. This will give you a few minutes away from the irritant that's causing your discomfort. Comb your hair, put on fresh makeup, splash water on your face, take a few deep breaths, have a smoke—do anything that'll help you to relax. It might help to recall an enjoyable experience. A vacation, a nice romance, a madcap evening out, even your favorite book or movie. Think pleasant thoughts for a few moments. Conjure up a peaceful image, a sailboat on a quiet lake, a mother hugging a child. Then hold these images in your mind and heart and rejoin the scene. But don't escape. A Tension Break is not an excuse to flee. It is only an opportunity to rest.

"Aha!" you may say. But, what if I'm in a car that's going 60 m.p.h.? How do I beat a hasty retreat then? Easy. The same way. Relax by *imagining* your leaving the scene. Picture yourself taking a nap or reading a book or sitting in a quiet room in a rocking chair.

Why should you take these real or imagined breaks? Because when you clam up, you tend to try too hard. While you may think you have failed miserably, what's really happening is that you've exhausted yourself attempting to be sociable. Removing yourself from the source of your tension helps you gather your forces and regain your stamina.

These are just a few of the techniques you can use when you start to clam up. Or, try desensitization exercises. Or invent some techniques of your own. The important thing is not to let a moment's panic destroy an entire evening. With the exercises developed for you here, you can easily weather a few minutes discomfort and quite possibly rise above them to wonderful new heights. *Bonne chance.*

31

Desensitizing Your Shyness

WOULD YOU believe some people could be so shy that they get physically ill when entering a party? Would you believe that some shy people get so nervous that they lose their voices when speaking on the phone? And would you believe that for some people the feelings caused by shyness are so overwhelming, they actually faint.

Well, it happens. In fact physical maladies and negative manifestations of shyness are quite common. Some shy friends are so terrified to approach or call an opposite-sex acquaintance that they often experience total voice loss, severe heart-pounding, uncontrollable sweating, constricted throat, and even fainting. For the severely shy the most common type of social intercourse can lead to a literal state of panic.

Shy people who feel sickeningly nervous when meeting new people or talking to strangers have never learned to properly discharge tension. Their anxiety mounts to a fever pitch . . . they get to the point of overload. Some people actually do faint. For shy people like these a very helpful technique is desensitization.

Desensitization is a term that has become popular among psychologists and laymen alike. So popular, in fact, and used so loosely that few people are sure what it actually means anymore.

Desensitization is a therapeutic device commonly used to treat phobias in a clinical setting. The therapist asks the patient to describe his or her particular fear and then makes a list of ten anxiety-causing situations related to that fear. For instance, a shy person may have a tremendous fear of meeting people. For that person the list would begin with "saying hello to a co-worker in the office"—the least anxiety-causing situation. Next he or she might say "looking a stranger in the face and saying hello." The list would progress to the last item which might be "entering a room full of strangers at a party and introducing myself to the group as a whole"—the most anxiety-causing situation.

The therapist takes the patient through each step of this "anxiety hierarchy" and teaches him to relax whenever a feeling of tenseness or nervousness begins to mount. The goal is to show the patient, the shy person in this case, how to keep from panicking in the most anxiety-causing situation.

Desensitization has been very effective in treating fears associated with meeting and talking to new people. However, it can be a long and laborious process involving many sessions with a therapist. It would hardly be practical to give a detailed explanation of it here.

Because of this, Dr. Renée Saltoun, a clinical psychologist and expert in desensitization, has developed a system of "self-desensitization" for the shy, especially for this book. This system can be used by shy people in virtually any anxiety-causing situation. Dr. Saltoun's system will help a shy person to relax. Once that is achieved a shy person can appear calm, comfortable, and self-assured in any social or nonsocial setting. The feelings of panic can be eliminated.

What happens when you are on a first date with that gorgeous guy in your apartment building? You're probably nervous and excited; that's natural, anyone would feel that way. But perhaps it's even worse than that for you. You are unable to look at his face. When you do talk, you blush. Your thoughts are directed inward; you're self-conscious, always thinking about how you look, how you're acting, and what you should say. You wonder if your eyelashes are on straight, if your perfume is too strong, if you are boring, or if you are being too formal. You become very anxious and perhaps panic sets in. Eventually you've totally tuned yourself out from your date and your surroundings.

By learning to relax a shy person can put an end to "shyness thoughts"—the constant feelings of negativism, self-criticism, and self-doubt. Just the act or process of trying to relax is sufficient to distract shy persons from thoughts about themselves. When that happens the attention and interest can move outward to the people the shy person is with.

Even in the most anxiety-causing situation, shy persons can put themselves in a state of relaxation. In effect, they learn to *role-play the part of a relaxed person.* A shy person who can act relaxed, who can talk and laugh and feel and love without tension and anxiety, is a person who can successfully act unshy. And remember, that's all that's needed for a good social life. You can feel as shy and lousy as you always feel, but if you can project the image of someone who is *not shy*, you are in actuality not shy.

How, you're wondering, will you ever learn to relax? The mere sight of a man makes your heart pound and your throat get tight. Saying hello to the girl in the flower shop leaves you blushing and feverish. A nod from the waiter or waitress at the luncheontte causes your hands to shake uncontrollably. You can't imagine any way to relieve the quivering mass of fear and shyness that is you.

Well, desensitization can help you get relief. Here is a typical situation perfect for using the desensitization technique.

You're a young woman working as an assistant manager at a

bank. You're able to hide your shyness by immersing yourself in your work. You have a cordial but not particularly close relationship with many of the other bank employees. One day the manager announces he's having a big retirement party for Georgette, a teller who has been with the bank for thirty years. You hesitate, but you see no way to get out of going. Besides, you've been so lonely lately part of you is tempted.

The evening of the party you are frightfully nervous. You haven't been to a social function in six months (the last was your sister's wedding which you couldn't avoid). When you get there, the room is filled with strangers and you actually feel ill as you ask the bartender for a drink. You sit on a couch in the corner that isolates you from the other guests.

Suddenly you notice a handsome man staring at you from across the room. You recognize him as a clerk in the administrative department. You glance away quickly, hoping he will not approach you. When you look up again you see him coming toward you. He sits next to you and says hello. You freeze in fear.

This scene is typical of many that shy people, in terror, have described. You know what happens next: the tightness in the chest, the sweaty palms, the feverish face, the nauseated feeling in the stomach, and the wild urge to turn and run. There is, however, a way to ease these feelings. Desensitization, in fact, acts to *interrupt* the state of shyness.

When you feel the tension mount, as in the situation above, sit with your back against the back of the chair, head erect, hands in a relaxed position but not touching. If you're standing, lift yourself up a little straighter with your head held erect. From this position you can begin the relaxation process. Two are described here, either of which you can use with equal effectiveness:

1.   Concentrate on one area of the body; usually the stomach works well. Allow all your weight to fall into the middle of your lower abdomen. Push all your upper body weight into

that one point. This is called one-pointedness. You'll notice your shoulders drop and your neck muscles relax. Feel your weight in your abdomen and keep it there until you regain composure. Then resume conversation or activity.

2.   Take a very deep breath through your nostrils. Imagine a tiny thread passing into your nose, through your neck, down your back and into your lower abdomen. When the thread gets to your stomach, hold it there for five seconds, then begin to exhale slowly. Repeat the exhalation up through the back, neck, et cetera, and let the air out through your mouth. This exercise should last about thirty seconds.

If at any time the anxiety is so intense that you are panicked and totally unable to start the above exercises, then don't fight that panic. Recognize the tension, let it last for a few seconds, and, when it begins to subside, then start the relaxation process.

Use these desensitization techniques as often as needed. Anytime you feel the shyness thoughts starting; anytime the self-criticism, self-condemnation, or self-judgment begins is the time to use desensitization. You will notice that the tension doesn't always disappear immediately. Sometimes you'll begin to feel relaxed, return to your activity, then the tension will start again. In that case, just repeat the desensitization technique.

Don't worry about the fact that you know you're using a desensitization technique. Recognizing that you're using a device to ease your tension in no way reduces the effectiveness of the technique. Remember, desensitization is designed to distract you from your shyness thoughts, relieve your tension, and allow you to relax.

You can use desensitization whenever you feel tense. The shyness thoughts are always destructive and self-defeating, and thinking them has become a habit for you. But the more you use desensitization, the less the thoughts haunt you and the more relaxed you are. You begin to decondition your shyness until you're no longer playing the role of a relaxed person—you *are* a relaxed person. And you can easily act unshy. Dr. Saltoun says that pathways in the mind atrophy from disuse. Wouldn't it be nice if you could stop the shyness thoughts forever by helping their pathways atrophy from disuse? You can!

Yes, desensitization *can* work for you. Once you feel relaxed in social situations you'll also *feel more sociable*. You will no longer experience fear and panic. You'll be able to talk with people easily, comfortably, and with genuine interest. No matter how shy you are *desensitization can help you act unshy*.

32

Little Crutches

IF EVER there were a strange notion expressed by shy people, it's that social affairs must be approached with a stoic sense of self-denial, denial of the so-called "little crutches" that can help to lessen a shy person's anxiety in social as well as nonsocial situations.

What exactly is a little crutch? Basically, it's anything (a prop that's carried around, some relatively harmless routine or habit, an article of clothing) that makes a person feel more comfortable, more attractive, more capable, more confident, more self-assured, and generally more willing and able to enter mildly threatening situations.

Paulette is a very shy young woman who has a glass of sherry, her "little crutch", while she's getting dressed for a date. She says it relaxes her, leaves her feeling a little less uptight about her makeup and hair, a little looser of tongue, a little lighter in spirit. When her date rings the buzzer Paulette glides toward the door already feeling close and friendly toward him, not as stiff and formal and grim as she used to feel when a date came to call. Of course, for some people, drinking to relax probably is hazardous, a habit that could lead them inescapably down the road to a slavish dependence on liquor. But there are millions of others who use social drinking to enhance their good times with absolutely no negative side effects at all. Alcoholic beverages *can* be used sanely, wisely, and profitably. And if you're the kind of person who finds that liquor relaxes you when ordinarily you'd be uptight and shy, *and* at the same time are confident that you have no tendency to become overly dependent on the stuff, then go ahead and have a drink before a party or a date or a dance. Since it's not doing anyone any harm there's no reason not to use every advantage you can.

In this book you've been asked to do some things that are difficult, challenging, downright terrifying. At the same time the book has tried to be supportive. It's traumatic and stressful overcoming shyness. There's no need to make it any more painful by denying yourself the crutches that somehow make you feel more secure, less vulnerable. So if you have little habits or props that you feel will help in your battle with shyness, by all means use them.

Following is a sort of catalogue of little crutches that shy people have used with success while meeting and dating new people. Maybe some of them will work for you. Remember, your crutches should somehow be related to your interests or needs, or they will seem ridiculous and may make you feel *more* uncomfortable. So don't wear an eye patch just because you like the way it looks on Moshé Dayan. Choose something that will truly help you, be a crutch for you, when dealing socially with others.

1. A camera—One young man carries an esoteric looking Leica with him at all times. His profession is retailing, and photography's not even his hobby. The reason he's

never without his Leica is that several years ago while walking through a park in San Francisco a friendly college student asked if he'd take her picture. They wound up spending the summer together. The young man reports that ever since, he's never fet truly comfortable without a camera on his person. Maybe a Nikon or Pentax would do the same for you. Then again maybe you'd feel it just isn't you. Think about it.

2. Cigarettes—They may not be healthy but some shy people can't live without them. If you're shy to begin with, leaving your cigarettes behind as you head out for your first date in three months would probably be more self-destructive than smoking itself. So go ahead, bring your weeds along tonight and make a vow that as soon as you conquer your shyness you're going to kick the habit.

3. A stopwatch—One very shy, inward assistant producer always carries a stopwatch around her neck. At first it appeared she was just showing off. But when she explained that without it she can never think of anything to talk about, there was little reason to be critical. She says it's great at parties or just riding the bus to work because people always ask her about it, and it gives her something very concrete and comfortable about which to talk.

4. Business card—This is one of the best little crutches in the whole wide world. If you don't work at a regular job have cards made up with your name, address, and phone number in the form of a business card. If your company hasn't supplied you with any, have a batch made up yourself. Many shy people cast their cards upon the water constantly and report that they've received more interested calls from truly desirable lovemates than they'd ever anticipated.

5. College sweatshirts, etc.—Some shy people like to wear a club blazer, or a club tie, or a T-shirt that says Philadelphia Track Club, or West Hartford Marathon, or

some saying or insignia on their clothes that identifies them as belonging to a certain group. If that's you, by all means do it. It can get a lot of conversations off the ground that otherwise would have stayed there.

6. Buttons—Some people wear a Save-the-Whale button. Other people wear Democrat, Republican, or Anti-nuclear Power buttons. These, too, can be excellent little crutches, especially for the very shy.

7. Miscellaneous—One shy friend uses a cane although his legs are fine. A woman in Manhattan carries a fine Italian fold-up umbrella which she uses to underscore points she makes in conversation. Another acquaintance always wears a beret, Tam o'Shanter, or other interesting hat. And yet another carries a hard rubber hand strengthener for his golf game. There are hundreds of others not mentioned that will work just as well for you.

Do you have a little crutch which helps make a social or romantic encounter that much easier, smoother, pleasanter to live through? Well, then don't leave it home. There are some people who feel they must be spartan, pure, never weak, never needful, never dependent. Nonsense. Anything that helps get you over the shyness hump, which isn't destructive to yourself or others, is good and healthy and should be exploited to the fullest.

33

Moving On

WHY IS it that so many shy people find it virtually impossible to walk out of a party, bar, restaurant, or dance, when it obviously holds no social promise for them? While confident, assertive persons can take one look into a party or discotheque and know whether to invest their time or move on, shy people seem reluctant to leave a social function even after it's become obvious the affair holds no prospect for romance. Here is a little rule all shy people should remind themselves of before they go out: YOU ARE OBLIGATED TO NO ONE BUT YOURSELF. YOU OWE NO ONE ANYTHING. BUT YOU OWE YOUR-SELF A FAIR CHANCE TO MEET SOMEONE SPECIAL.

Listen, shy people, you can't stay at the same depressing social affair hour after hour if there are no people for you to meet or if everyone's taken! You have to keep moving. Let's say you've been invited to a party. You walk in, get something to drink, and find (if you're a woman, for example) that there are only four men there. One is wearing a gold wedding band, the second is a radical priest, another is obviously gay, and the fourth is taken— by the gay guy. What do you do? One thing you could do is pat yourself on the back for making it out of the house and then just sit in a quiet corner all evening nibbling peanuts and studying album covers. After all, it would be so comfortable. Don't do that. Instead, stay for a polite but very short time, thank the host or hostess, and leave. Go find a discotheque. Wander into a bar. Go anywhere, but keep moving until you find a place with some social promise. Yes, this is easier said than done, but keep the idea in mind before you leave your home for the evening. Then you'll be prepared to take the necessary action. If you've conditioned yourself ahead of time to move on if the going gets dull, you'll find it easier to spot the telltale signs of dullness and to beat a hasty retreat.

Think of it this way: You've made an investment. You're dressed, you're primed to have a good time, and you got yourself out the door. Is it your fault that the party, dance, dinner turned out to be a crashing bore? Before you leave your home to go out, what you should do is put a list in your pocket or bag of places you could go as backups. Go to your first destination, and if you see there's nothing for you there, cross that off your list and move on. Keep moving, even if it means hitting three places all in one evening.

Here are certain hints that will make this easier for you:

1. Leave the house with enough money to get around. That way expenses won't hold you back if you decide to move on.
2. Pick places that are close to each other or at least in the same part of town. That will save you time and money.
3. Wear a watch. Know that the evening will not go on forever and that if you wait until midnight to make a move, people will have begun to pair off.
4. Take a car. If you don't drive and you think you might move around, go with a friend who's a "mover," and make sure that friend has a car. If that's not possible,

know how to make connections with public transportation.

Let's say you're away on business or on vacation. You're going to have dinner in a restaurant alone. Before you let anyone seat you at a table, get a good idea of who is sitting at the other tables. If it looks like a convention of the Gray Panthers, while they may charm you, you probably won't want to date them. The same goes for a good seat on a plane. Make sure you get the seat you want. An aisle seat is the best because there's more scanning room to spot someone interesting.

So, if you don't like the restaurant, leave. If you're not satisfied with your seat on the plane, change it. If the party is dull, cut out. All you have to say is: "Thank you very much but I've changed my mind," "I don't like this seat," or "I have to leave now." It is hard for shy persons to fight their sick feelings when confronted with the arched eyebrows, down-turned mouth, or look of "genuine" disappointment from the host, flight attendant, or maitre d'. But you must simply move on anyway.

In the type of social situations just described, you are dealing, for the most part, with strangers. Outside of common courtesy you don't owe them a thing. You must be ruthlessly selfish. Your first obligation is to yourself, just as their first obligation is to themselves. If you want to change your mind or move on, go ahead and do it. Your goal is fun and romance, not to be liked by the whole human race.

You should try to get the most mileage possible out of any situation with social potential. There's an art to doing that. Take pride in the thought that you had the guts to get out of the house and do whatever it is you're doing. Remind yourself that you deserve to have a good time doing it. Your body should be ready to pick itself up and move on wherever necessary because having a good time and meeting people is your prime objective. Like a good friend in San Francisco always says in his special way, "If it ain't happenin' downtown, get your ass uptown." Right on!

34

Rejection Is Good for You

GETTING REJECTED is painful, embarrassing, and makes you want to hide in a closet and never come out again. So how can it possibly be *good* for you? The answer is profoundly simple. If you're not being rejected, it's a sign you're doing nothing to conquer your shyness. And if you're doing nothing to conquer your shyness, that's bad. Real bad. Because it's just not going to get any better all by itself.

Rejection triggers so many emotional buttons, most shy people consider it a dirty word. It means loss, loneliness, and a lowering of self-esteem. You probably think it is to be avoided at all costs. In fact, if you want to be a little truthful with yourself, wouldn't you admit that more than half the times you stayed in instead of going out were because of Fear of Rejection?

The advice and exercises in this book have been structured so that they lead you gradually toward taking chances, making little forrays into the world of dating and dancing and partying. But the fact is, and you know it, that sooner or later you're going to have to do something that's going to put your pride and feelings on the line. You're going to have to phone that gorgeous lawyer in the next office and ask him over for a special home-cooked dinner. You're going to have to stroll right up to that statuesque redhead at your local disco and ask her to dance. There's no getting around it. Attractive, interesting lovemates aren't going to appear in your life through magic. And the reality is that not everybody you ask to date and dance and be with you is going to say yes. Some are going to say no. Maybe not a lot of them, maybe only a very few, but some will definitely say no. And the big question is, how are you going to deal with it? Are you going to curl up into the fetal position, stick your thumb in your mouth, and never venture out of your room again? Or are you going to continue living, winning some, losing some, forging ahead like most people? You see, that's one of the traits that distinguishes the very shy from the not-so-shy. Everyone gets rejected. Shy people go to pieces over it, while not-so-shy people carry on.

It's astonishing how many people over the years have confided in a whisper, "You know what my problem is? I'm afraid of being rejected." They say this as if they were talking about a rare jungle disease rather than a feeling shared by every reasonably sane human being on earth. Everyone's afraid of being rejected as well as afraid of getting hit by cars and caught in the rain and mugged and of catching cold and so on and so on. But in order to get any enjoyment out of life you have to forge on through your fears, live with them, experience them, and quite often fall victim to them. It's part of the life process.

Darwin discovered that tension and hostility in an environment is necessary to the survival of a species. If a particular animal or plant is allowed to develop unchallenged, if its food and water supply are abundant, if it never has to fight or struggle to stay alive, it crumples at the very first sign of adversity. Without rejection, a person could die. Literally. Think of it this way. Imagine what would happen if a particularly shy young woman chose never to open herself up to a possible rejection. Instead of going out to dances and singles bars and parties she commutes from her apartment to work and back to her apartment. She dreams of a handsome man who will come up to her desk or approach her on the bus to work. But it never happens. Year after year goes by without any luck. Before she knows it, she's forty-five years old and growing quieter and shyer and more inward by the day, less capable of ever getting out of herself again. By the time she's fifty she realizes she will never marry, never live with a man, and never have anyone to share her bed. At this point, who stands a better chance of staying alive? A woman of the same age who's spent the last thirty years getting her share of rejections but at least has a boyfriend or two, perhaps a husband, and certainly a social network of men and women friends to have lunch with, dinner with, to spend weekends with; or the woman who has retreated more and more into herself and lives in an interior world?

Again, this point isn't intended to depress you but simply to convince you that there is nothing very poetic or charming about an overdeveloped fear of rejection. In a very young child it may be cute. In an adult, it's sad.

Well, what can you do about it then? How can you overcome this terrible, paralyzing, self-defeating fear? One thing you can do is: LOOK UPON REJECTION AS VICTORY.

The more you get rejected the better you're doing in your battle to defeat shyness. Some people get so many rejections in one year they feel like pin cushions or particularly hated voodoo dolls. But you know something? It sure inures them to those nasty words: "Oh, gee, I'm sorry, but I'm busy that night." After a while they get so they can stand their ground, take a deep breath, and say, "Well, what about *next* Saturday night? No? Then how about the one after that?" They can stay on the phone for nearly an hour talking a reluctant old acquaintance from high school into coming to a party that started fifteen minutes ago. Rejection really can build strength.

Can you learn to look at getting rejected as a victory? You won't be deceiving yourself if you do. For shy people it really is a victory for it means that they've temporarily won the retreat-advance battle that is constantly going on inside every shy person. Remember, there's nothing to be ashamed of when you get rejected. If you are rejected, it doesn't necessarily say anything about you. Have you ever considered that the person you're asking out may be so painfully shy that he or she *is not able* to accept your invitation? At least you've had the courage to challenge your shyness, and you'll learn and grow as much from a rejection as an acceptance. You're just going through something that is a natural part of life.

Five years ago the author spent some time in Los Angeles filming a commercial with a famous fullback in the National Football League. One night after dinner and drinks, the football player began approaching every woman with whom he came in contact. He was well-dressed, reasonably sober, handsome, tall, and well-built. And yet each of the women he approached turned him down. It was hard to figure out what he was doing wrong. Perhaps he was too confident, too cocky. Perhaps it just wasn't his night. The important thing to note, however, is that he was rejected, time after time after time. And he just kept trying. So rejection happens to everyone, even famous football players, and it's crucial for you to understand that it is not a sign of your unworthiness, your inferiority, your *differentness* if someone turns you down. Rather, it's a sign of your health, your normalcy, your humanity.

The author did a radio show in New York City last year on shyness and meeting people. Midway through the show a blind college student called up. He explained he was currently dating three girls at once and sleeping with all of them. He wanted to know if the author thought this was okay from a moral standpoint. The author was stunned, not because of this man's promiscuity, but at his having three women who were willing to sleep with him. The author asked him as tactfully as possible how he managed to have such an active social life. The blind student said that he asks just about every girl he meets if she'll go out with him.

"I get a hell of a lot of turndowns," he said, "but I also meet a lot of girls who are quite happy to go out with me."

You think you've got it tough because you're shy? You say you're afraid of being rejected? Imagine how much more trepidation you'd have if you were disabled on top of it. Yet here is a twenty-year-old college student who opens himself up to five and six rejections a day and is still in there pitching, doing battle with life. Next time you feel yourself retreating and avoiding an encounter, think of the bravery of that young blind man. And see if you can't follow in his footsteps. If you get rejected, so what! You're doing a hell of a lot better than all those other shy people hiding in their rooms.

If you're in a situation where you sense that a rejection is imminent, don't suddenly fall apart. There are two basic ways to face a rejection, with a negative attitude or a positive attitude. You have a choice, and it's just as easy to choose the positive as it is the negative (although you no doubt have chosen the negative for years). The positive attitude is the crispest, most efficient way to dispense with rejection and move on without looking back. Here are three scenes involving rejection in which we present both attitudes on How to Be Rejected:

THE LEAST PAINFUL REJECTION

"Hi, what's that you're drinking?"

"Gin and tonic."

"How about bringing it outside where it's cooler and we can talk?"

"I'd rather not."

You have just been rejected. She (or he) does not want to join you.

Negative Attitude: No wonder, she (or he) won't come with me. I'm too fat and I have ears that stick out and I'm shy and I didn't make my approach right. I guess I'll finish this drink and go home. I feel depressed. It was a stupid idea to come here anyway.

Positive Attitude: Boy, is that person missing out. I'm nice and kind and I listen well. I'm not going to let this rejection knock me out. I have to relax and try again.

A MORE PAINFUL REJECTION

"Hi, Sue, this is Arnold. We met at that party last night and you gave me your phone number so I'm calling. I was wondering if you wanted to go out Saturday night?"

"Sorry, I'm busy."

"Well, what about next Saturday night?"

"Sorry, busy then, too."

Negative Attitude: Well, what the hell did she bother to give me her phone number for? She must have decided I'm shy or one of her girlfriends told her not to bother with me. Why do I take a girl's number in the first place? They act interested, then they don't want to go out when you call them. There's really something wrong with me.

Positive Attitude: Well, this isn't so bad. Maybe she was going with someone and went back with him. Or, maybe she gave me her phone number and then had second thoughts about going out with me. A lot of women do that. Because, at the time, she's flattered and doesn't know how to say no. At least she didn't mix up the digits and give me the wrong number. Okay, who needs her. It's a free country. I'll call another woman.

A MOST PAINFUL REJECTION

"Hi, Bob, this is Carol. Haven't heard from you for two weeks and I was thinking about you. I remember you said you felt like you were getting sick or something . . ."

"Well, uh, er, I've been busy."

"Maybe you'd like to come to dinner Saturday night?"
"Well, uh, er, I'm going out of town."

Negative Attitude: Oh, God, I'm going to die. Why did I ever sleep with him? (Or, why didn't I sleep with him?) How do you like that? Four dates and he just stops calling—no reason, no nothing. It's because I'm too shy and not sexy. Why would anyone bother with me? How could I have made such a fool out of myself to call him up? I hate men. I'm not going to take chances like this again.

Positive Attitude: I'm going to have a glass of wine and call my dearest friend and talk this out. He could have at least had the courtesy to say he wasn't interested. Well, I don't care. I'm glad this happened now. If he doesn't want to get to know me better, he doesn't know what he's missing. I'm a good person. But, right now, it hurts a little. So, I'm going to do what I have to do and then forget this character and go out Saturday night and have some fun. There're other fish in the sea. I've learned something from that phone call. The next one will be easier.

If these rejections and reactions seem all too familiar, it's because all of these things have happened to shy people who have faced rejection. These are the common, ordinary rejections that come up in a dating career. They're good for you. Think of them as steps you have to climb toward being self-assured socially. But, you can only grow that thicker skin by learning to take the positive attitude and shedding the negative one. Go out and chalk up a few rejections. That's the only way it will work. In the book of your life this kind of rejection doesn't even merit a paragraph because, in time, you'll forget how you felt.

This chapter could be considered the tip of an iceberg on the subject of rejection. Psychologists have said that the reason rejection triggers off various emotional buttons in different people goes back to childhood. When someone says, "I can't go out with you," you are actually *feeling* something that had the power to hurt you very deeply when you were an innocent child and couldn't understand or protect yourself.

But, basically, it comes down to this:

1. Rejection is not a dirty word and doesn't have to be.
2. In time a rejection will affect you less and less.
3. Living through a rejection is the only way to put it and keep it in its place. And it's a natural part of social growth.
4. Take a positive attitude toward rejection.

Think of rejection not as a personal chord that when struck sends you vibrating to hell and back but rather as . . . just one of those things you can learn to live with. Go out and practice living and loving and you'll learn something you won't find in a book. Rejection becomes an insignificant part of your life once you learn to feel more confident.

35

Seize the Day

CARL IS a young man who works for a huge corporation in a prestigious position and is very competent in his job. Although socially he is quite shy, he easily deceives a lot of people because he is confident and assertive in business. They assume that he is the same way about dating and sex.

One morning at work Carl stood in line at the coffee machine and noticed that right in front of him was a new employee, Sharon. She worked in the public relations department. He'd noticed her before when she'd been introduced around and thought she was very attractive. He wasn't positive but he had the feeling that she had smiled at him whenever they had passed each other in the halls.

On this particular morning Sharon began talking to him the instant Carl nodded hello. She debated the merits of the chocolate-covered doughnut versus the corn muffin, and she also started talking about the weather and her cat. All Carl could think of at the time was, "Oh-my-gosh, she's so pretty and has such a great personality. I really like her. I should ask her out, damn it. It's Tuesday, I could ask her out for Saturday night right now. No, I can't do that. She probably has a date. She's probably living with someone. To think that she singled me out to smile at and talk with, well, that's stupid. She smiles at everyone. After all, she's in public relations; that's how she got the job. She doesn't really like me. Anyway, by tomorrow I'll have a date for Saturday night, so it doesn't matter."

Carl didn't ask her out. She got the corn muffin and went back to her office. When Saturday night rolled around, sure enough, he didn't have a date. He was just as lonely and alone as ever and he couldn't stop thinking about Sharon. He should have asked her out right then and there in the coffee line. If only he could have a second chance!

Someone, somewhere, must have heard his wish. Two weeks later, he got his second chance. Sharon was right near him in the coffee line again. Remembering how miserable he had been that Saturday night and how he had wished for just one more chance, he blurte out, "Say, Sharon, what about lunch today?" "Sure," she answered, "I'd love to." Walking back to his office, Carl could hardly believe his luck. He'd gotten the words out and she'd accepted. Their lunch went really well and he didn't feel shy with her at all. They got along marvelously and are going together to this day.

The point of this anecdote is simple. There are very few times when life presents a romantic chance experience. Furthermore, if you are shy, it is difficult for you to recognize one because you are nervous; your social antennae are not sensitive to these experiences. But, if you do sense a little spontaneous magic between you and someone else, realize that it is a great gift. This is not a moment to throw away because you're not going to get very many of them. Grab it and do something . . . seize the day.

These magical moments will happen to you from time to time simply because you're a person walking around San Francisco or

Atlanta or Cleveland or New York or Middleberg or wherever. Every now and then, who knows where or when, you're going to be thrown up against someone magical whether you're at a party, in an office, on a bus or train, or even in a crowded elevator. You're going to feel a special spark, a chemistry, a magnetic vibration that's very real.

Whenever that happens, don't let negative doubts drag you down. Don't give it a second thought. It's happening to you! Once Bridget was getting off a bus loaded down with bundles and parcels when she bumped into someone and the packages went flying. Bending down to pick everything up, she was aware of someone trying to help her, mumbling apologies as he did so. She straightened up and found herself eyeball to eyeball with one of the most attractive men she'd ever seen in her life. If she could draw a picture of her "type," there he was. Her heart began to pound, her pulse raced, her eyelashes fluttered. It was one of those magical moments supplied by fate. And Bridget seized it. "Um, look, could you please lend me a hand?" she somehow managed to get out. "I live just up the block."

The man seemed only too glad to help. Before they got to Bridget's apartment, he suggested they stop in at an intimate pub for a glass of wine. The romance lasted for six wonderful, delightful months. All because Bridget had managed to get up her courage and say something.

These magic moments come few and far between. Unlike Carl, most people do not get a second chance. So if you feel a special attraction to someone fate sends your way, don't assume he is smiling or being nice just because he's that way with everyone. Assume that you've been singled out and take action. In these situations you can start a conversation with the most basic sort of small talk. These moments are magical when they come your way. Seize them.

36

Learning the Art of Harmless Kidding

SINCE DULL and boring dates are a common complaint among shy people, another suggestion that can break the sullen mood, which often seizes the moment and deadens it, is called the art of harmless kidding.

The art of harmless kidding is just that—kidding a date or friend in a harmless, gentle sort of way. Harmless kidding is always done jokingly, in jest, and *never nastily*. It is a light, tongue-in-cheek way to tell someone you feel playful and enjoy his or her company.

You're probably saying, "Oh no, that's for someone else. Impossible for me." Well, just try it once. If you're a woman and you're out with a guy wearing wing-tipped shoes, look down at them and say, "What are all those little holes on your shoes for? Do they air out your feet?" There will probably be a slight pause while he catches on, and then a cheerful laugh. If you're a man and you're out with a woman, pick something she's wearing that's outrageously fashionable and poke fun at it. If she has a popular frizzy hairdo, for instance, ask if the lights in her apartment have been growing dim. When she looks at you questioningly, say, "It's just that it looks like your hair has been soaking up all the electricity."

Before your next date, or the next time you see a friend, spend a few minutes thinking about things about him that might lend themselves to a little harmless kidding. Then practice how you might say it in a cheerful, friendly, innocent way—the tone of your voice is crucial. You want them to know you're having fun *with* them, not making fun *of* them. There's a big difference.

Perhaps you're amazed that this book would even suggest such a thing to you. After all, you're a shy person and shy people are sensitive, careful, would never risk angering a date or jeopardizing a relationship by kidding. The point is, however, that harmless kidding has the opposite effect and rarely angers a date at all. To the contrary, it helps people warm up to you and enjoy your company more. People simply *love* to be kidded because it says you've noticed them. People are used to being kidded. Just walk into any business office. Or consider your relationships with same-sex friends. People kid and poke fun at each other constantly. It is like a running game that loosens people up and breaks the monotony and formality of a business office or any other environment. Kidding works in a mysterious way to endear people to you.

Roger is a good friend who sells industrial real estate and is enormously successful. But ten years ago he was the low man at a small real estate firm, barely making enough in commissions to survive. It was a strange thing. Around his friends Roger was an exciting, amiable, playful guy who was always kidding and joking around. Everyone loved him. He was the life of every party.

But in his office it was like black and white, Dr. Jekyll and Mr. Hyde. Roger was a different person. He was quiet, reserved, inhibited. He never kidded around with office buddies, and he seemed to have a cold, formal rapport with everyone. It was amazing; a guy who was a social animal at night became a shy and timid creature during the day.

When it was mentioned to Roger how surprising his stiff, unsmiling office demeanor was, he said he thought that was the way he was supposed to act at work. He thought his boss would be angry if he joked around, so he maintained a somber profile around the firm.

After Roger was convinced that his skill at harmless kidding was one of his most attractive qualities, he slowly began to loosen up. Within a week he reported that he had made friends, both male and female, with several people who had never talked to him before. Everyone, including his boss, was wondering where he suddenly got his great sense of humor.

Today Roger is constantly hobnobbing with the presidents of large corporations, and they all adore him. All these austere, silent big businessmen cling to Roger for one reason—he kids them. These stuffy fellows are thrilled when someone jokes with them. It's something their employees seem to never have the nerve to attempt.

Roger simply was born with the gift of harmless kidding. Or he might have learned it from a parent. He can make lofty, corporate presidents laugh at themselves and they love it. He'll gawk at their huge, chauffeured limousines and quip, "Gee, you think the three of us can fit in there?" Or he'll look at their somber, dark suits and say, "Wow, you sure are a wild dresser, Mr. McDermott." Whatever the comment, it's said in a playful, gentle way.

You can utilize this technique as easily as Roger does. The next time an evening out becomes a formal occasion, or you suddenly feel transformed into a walking, talking wooden puppet, try some harmless kidding. It can act to release your tension and relax you. If you're apprehensive, practice the technique with relatives, co-workers, or same-sex friends before you try it on a date. Chances are you already do kid to some degree with people with whom you're comfortable.

But be very careful with the tone and intention of your voice when kidding. If you practice on your aunt by remarking that her legendary rhubarb pie tastes a little rubbery, and you notice she's close to tears, you'd better perfect your technique.

You can also listen to how other people kid. You'll be astonished at how often harmless kidding is used in conversation. It may seem unthinkable now, but once you try it, you'll find how much people enjoy being kidded. Simple, harmless kidding can make you the type of person people want to be near—even if you're shy!

37

Spontaneous Silliness

DURING COUNSELING sessions with shy people at least one suggestion always meets with horror, disbelief, or incredulity. More than any other, the suggestion to act "silly" with the opposite sex is the most frightening. Silliness is impossible . . . a truly unthinkable act.

"If I act silly," shy friends say, "I'll make a fool out of myself. It won't seem funny; it will seem maniacal." Or "my silliness would just draw attention to me and my date would be ill with embarrassment. I'd never get another date in my life."

These concerns, of course, are exaggerated and unrealistic. When this is pointed out to shy people, citing countless cases of how "spontaneous silliness" helped to add laughter and fun to a date, there is a sudden changed expression—shy people seem tickled by the idea of being spontaneously silly. It's as if in the deep recesses of their minds they have always longed to be a little crazy, zany, or silly, but their shyness acts like an inhibitory policeman preventing any spontaneous gestures.

The fact is people don't want to go out with formal sticks of furniture or properly well-behaved lamp posts. That type of behavior makes everyone feel formal and stiff as well. People want to be with living, breathing men and women who laugh and cry and sweat and enjoy every moment of life. So the next time you're out with someone and you feel things are getting awfully dull, do something silly.

You don't have to be outrageous or embarrass yourself or turn yourself inside out. Just think back to the time you were a kid and had an urge to do some mischief. Then, break the silence or heaviness with something silly. Tell someone not to move because there's a spider on his shoulder. Ask the other person to go looking for UFO's with you. When you're walking on the street, challenge your friend to a footrace, or pluck a dandelion and stick it in his buttonhole. Do anything that strikes you as being a little zany.

You're probably remembering back to the last time you were with someone of the opposite sex. Maybe you remember being uncomfortable, quiet, dull. Where do you get the impetus to suddenly transform yourself into a Harpo Marx, if the date is already dragging and you're feeling low? The answer is, you don't need to feel happy or high to do something silly. You simply do it. Remember, the key to a happier love life is in learning to *act* outgoing. And doing something silly is indeed outgoing behavior. Think of it this way. If everything is sliding downhill anyway, what have you got to lose? Give it your best shot or your worst shot and it doesn't matter. The object is just to be silly.

Rather than have you spend an hour during your next date debating over an appropriately silly act, included here is a list of items. Naturally the best way to be spontaneous is to pull something from the Silly File Cabinet of your own mind. But if something on this list strikes you as being "perfect," go ahead. They've all been used with great success:

- If you wear glasses, or sunglasses, turn them upside down and continue talking normally.
- If you're out to dinner, distract the other person so he or she looks away, then switch plates.
- Launch a search for some kind of crazy food. Make it something wild like chicken tacos or leftover chocolate-covered Easter eggs in July. Make sure it's "kid" food and not elegant cuisine.
- If there is a park nearby with a fountain, suggest a foot dunking or even a swim.
- Buy ice cream cones for both of you. Make a big thing about how the ice cream smells funny. Ask, "Does it smell funny to you?" When he or she takes a sniff, gently push their nose into the ice cream.
- If you pass a trendy shop or antique boutique, insist on going in to try on crazy hats.
- Ask a silly question: "What person in history would you most like to have been?" or "Whom would you most like to be stranded on a desert island with?"
- Bring your date a silly little present, like a corn cob pipe or an all-day lollipop.
- Pick up a "water squirt" flower at a novelty shop. Not only can you use this on your date, but offer a fragrant squirt to your waiter or waitress, the ticket-taker at the theater, a salesperson at a store. Most everyone will react good-naturedly and you'll both have a laugh. Incidentally, novelty shops are filled with thousands of such silly gags that are harmless and can help a lot to loosen up a dull moment. Take a stroll through one of these shops and pick up an arsenal of any novelty items that tickle your fancy.
- If you're walking near a curb hop up on it and do a tight-rope act like one of the Great Wallendas.

These are just a few suggestions. Another good idea is to get the person talking about her childhood. Reminiscing about childhood pranks always make people feel a little childish and silly.

Keep in mind, it's no crime to be silly. In fact, spontaneous silliness is a great device to use when you're feeling yourself clamming up or becoming dull and boring. Nonshy people, both male and female, who have many successful relationships know how to act silly at the appropriate times. Acting silly can take an evening that is dropping like a bomb and bring it to the height of pleasure.

38

The Power of a Compliment

LIKE SMALL talk, the compliment is a powerful tool for a shy person. In fact, it is almost sinfully powerful because it is so easy to use and can bring such dynamic results. To develop your skills, you can compliment the people you meet as often as five to ten times a day (not the same person five times, of course, but five different people once).

A compliment works like magic. It is like manna to the soul. Presidents love compliments. No one is too lofty to adore a compliment. So if you feel an impulse to compliment, or even if you don't feel an impulse—try it. Tell a woman her hair looks terrific after she's just had it done. Tell a guy who shows up in a great-looking suit that you like his taste. Let someone know she has a great smile. You can't imagine the good feelings and warmth it will unlock for you.

Here is a good example of just how powerful a compliment

can be. This incident was witnessed in a coffee shop the other day. Standing in line waiting to pay her bill (the line was endless because it was lunchtime) was a young woman. She was fairly attractive. In front of her was a young man who kept turning around to look at her. The line was moving very slowly. Finally, the young man turned and said, "You know, you must be a country girl."

Silence. Surely some wisecrack or putdown on her part had to follow. Talk about a line! But surprisingly the woman smiled and blushed and said, "What makes you say that?"

The man, twinkling with friendliness and sincerity, replied, "Because you have such pink, rosy cheeks. I've been in the city all day and everyone looks so peaked. I haven't seen anyone with a complexion like yours since I was up in Vermont." Well, this young woman, who minutes before had been standing there looking bored, almost dissolved into a little pool of butter on the floor. She seemed touched. She immediately leaned closer to the man and began a conversation with him. She no longer looked just fairly attractive. She had become radiant, blooming.

You may not feel, so early in the game, like testing yourself by going up to a stranger and saying something as adventurous as the man in the coffee shop did. That's okay. But if the idea seems far-fetched now, one day *you* will be capable of doing much the same thing. For now, compliment people when it feels right, and do it often. Try to practice complimenting under the two following circumstances:

1. *Compliment a grouch.* That is, compliment someone who is really in a bad mood. It could be the clerk in the grocery store, the bank teller, a receptionist, or a bus driver. But it should be someone you don't know. Compliment them either on something you notice that is nice about their appearance or respond to an aspect of their job that looks difficult. Let them know you think they do it well.

2. *The next time you clam up, try a compliment.* It could be

at a party or with a date or even with same-sex friends. Use a compliment to help bring you back into the present. Without a doubt you'll elicit a positive response. This, in turn, helps you feel more comfortable in rejoining the conversation.

The above two exercises will help you to gain skills in complimenting strangers, the way the man in the coffee shop did. They will show you how effectively a compliment can be used to your advantage.

Don't feel that free or frequent complimenting is phony or manipulative. To the contrary. To withhold a compliment, a feeling of love, an impulse to touch a fellow human being either with hands or words, *this* is phony, manipulative, and a misguided attempt at keeping another from gaining power over you. This society has developed a mass stinginess, a games-people-play approach to keeping fellow men or women hungering for love and acceptance.

It is the person who has the courage to express his or her love and admiration for someone else, who is being honest and spontaneous, who is speaking truly from the heart. That is why a compliment has such an awesome ability to unleash the stored-up warmth lurking within everyone.

Dina, a bank executive, went out with Victor, a man from her office whom she really wasn't too attracted to. Someone once described Dina as having the looks of a beauty queen and the keen mind of a corporation president. Victor had a lesser job in another department and kept stopping by at Dina's office until she reluctantly agreed to go out with him, solely to tell him he was definitely not her type. She had planned to meet him after work and then go home and wash her hair and hop into bed with a good book.

Victor was chubby and starting to bald. Dina could imagine people saying, "What's she doing with him?" Victor took her to an elegant restaurant and ordered a bottle of the best wine. Then, halfway through dinner, he began to compliment her. He told her what silky hair she had, what deep, soulful eyes, what a velvety complexion, what a fine mind, what exquisitely sculpted hands, what a spiritually beautiful experience it would be to wake up and see her long, wavy hair spilling over the pillow next to him.

Victor wasn't being macho or crude or even sensual. In his genuine admiration his compliments became so lavish, Dina felt they were almost poetic. She began to feel tremendously sexually aroused.

You're probably saying, "Oh, c'mon, how could she fall for a line like that? So what if he was being sincere. If she wasn't attracted to him in the first place, how could drivel like that turn her on?" Well, therein lies the power of a compliment. To an observer at a nearby table, Victor's words may very well have sounded ludicrous. But when you are the one being complimented you often can't tell that you are the "snowee."

People wear blinders. They believe and accept and gush over every complimentary word said to them. By the way, capable, competent, smooth, smart Dina went home that night and made love to short, paunchy, balding Victor.

When she related the incident, she admitted that the love-making wasn't half as sensual and exciting as the poetry of his words. Nevertheless, the power of his compliments were such that they did turn her on, and she did go to bed with him.

Here's yet another anecdote which shows how a compliment is able to trigger a deep emotional, even sexual, response. A couple who live in Greenwich Village tell this funny story. One evening not too long ago the couple were getting ready for bed. The man was eager and ready for sex; the woman was not. She was exhausted from picking up after a rebellious three year old all day, and she gave her husband a firm no when he suggested they make love. She was too tired to even try to pretend an interest.

Just as an experiment, the husband began to toy with the power of the compliment. He told his wife that he had forgotten to tell her how lovely she had looked at the party they attended the previous night. Compared to the other women there, no one had come close to her special sparkle. She had looked young and fresh, even dewy. He had felt so proud of her, and had noticed how all the other men had looked her way.

His wife, who had been feeling bone-tired, began to feel extremely turned on. As the man's compliments escalated, so did her desire, until pretty soon they jumped into bed and made love. All because this man, her husband, to whom she had been married for ten years, had started complimenting her.

This is not to say that only men can turn on women with a compliment. Women can do it as well, with just a little more care. The results are not usually passionate lovemaking or even innocent passes. The women report that most men turn somewhat pink around the ears, thank them, and may say, "I'm flattered."

When you compliment a man, he will probably feel warm toward you. But because of *la difference*, he may look at the compliment as just that, a compliment, not a seduction ritual. So turn it into a prelude to sex by aiming your compliments not toward his IQ or business brilliance but square on his physical attributes. Tell him: "You have the most muscular arms. I think that's so sexy in a man." Then, with the cunning of a southern belle, cool it. A little later: "You know those little hairs peeking out from your shirt. That is just such a turn-on for me." In other words, direct a full assault couched in sexual terms, toward his body or masculinity. Don't be too obvious, but don't be too subtle. The more you sincerely and naturally compliment a man on anything you honestly appreciate about him, the easier it's going to be to get to know him well. He may look like you're punishing him, as his face screws up in a pained expression to consider the compliment, but don't let it throw you. He's thrilled! He loves it.

In its basic form a compliment can change a frown to a smile, remove a chip from someone's shoulder, make someone feel warm toward you. You can use a compliment to get just about anyplace you'd like to be with a person.

Now, of course, if you are going to compliment, you should do it as *honestly* and sincerely as possible. You don't have to make up something or tell a lie. How do you do this?

GET IN TOUCH WITH YOUR FEELINGS

What is it that you find attractive about someone? Everyone has something. What is it that you really find special? Is it her hair, eyes, smile, something about her personality? Search inside yourself for the "real" compliment. You don't just have to pick one out of a hat. Search for a compliment that is creative and honest. Find something you think is special about that person.

HOW TO TAKE A COMPLIMENT

There are some shy people who can't take compliments. Although they may be flattered on the inside, on the outside they act flustered. Many shy people go to pieces when they are complimented. Sometimes shy people are so ungracious about accepting a compliment that they inadvertently end up insulting the complimentor. Or they may giggle, stammer, look at the floor—even walk away as if they had been *insulted.*

Since it's as important to learn to take a compliment as it is to give one, try this simple exercise the next time you get a compliment: LOOK THE PERSON IN THE EYE AND SAY, "THANK YOU VERY MUCH. THAT'S NICE."

That's only six words. Learn them. The next time you get a compliment and you feel yourself going to pieces out of habit—stop, think, and bring to mind the six words. Memorize them, if you have to, and use them. It will say so much about you. For instance (1) it will say that you think well enough of yourself to accept the compliment; and (2) you are grateful and are thanking the person for extending himself to say something kind about you.

The effect of accepting a compliment well makes people like you better. The effect of giving a compliment well makes people like you better. In terms of power, a compliment is one of the mightiest weapons in the world—only it never does any harm.

39

Whatever Works

As YOU near the end of this book you're probably wondering, "How can I put all these ideas to work? There are so many suggestions, I'll never be able to remember them all!"

Well, you don't have to. Not everything in the book will work for you. You might be totally repulsed by the idea of going to a singles bar. Then don't, as long as you can replace that activity with some other social activity. But others *will* want to go to a singles bar, and for them there is included here a section on approaching people at these crowded, noisy, but sometimes very effective arenas for meeting.

Think of this book as a smorgasbord of antishyness techniques: It is a long table where you can take a taste of this, try a portion of that, serve yourself a sample from over there, or dip into a little something from over here. In the end you'll find a suggestion that you like, feel comfortable with, and most importantly, that works for you.

Perhaps there are many ideas in this book that you like. If that's the case, find the right moment and use them. If there are only a few ideas you feel comfortable with, use only those but use them frequently, until you have the confidence to try something a little more challenging.

Not everything in this book is going to work for everybody in the same way. While one shy person might feel that the creative compliment is the greatest device ever offered to the shy, another will insist that nothing is more beneficial than assertiveness training. That's fine. Almost every idea or suggestion in this book is powerful enough by itself to take you far in learning to act unshy. Each has been tried, tested, and found to be very effective in helping the shy feel more socially confident.

So be sure *to use whatever works.* Don't feel obligated to become spontaneously silly if you have succeeded in getting three dates by using positive projection. Stick with the thing that's working. Just make sure you do something. You've bought this book to help you with your shyness—let it help!

Before this book went to the publisher, a copy of the manuscript was given to a dozen of our shy friends. They offered their reactions to it, and at the same time they all were helped by it. One of the people, Irv, seemed extremely excited by it. "The book is great!" he said excitedly. "I got so psyched up by it I called this girl from work and asked her out that very night." That was to be Irv's first date in over four months. "It started fine. We went to dinner and a few times there was silence, but I just used some small-talk openers. Monique, the girl I was with, just loved the small talk. I think she could have talked all night. Then about ten o'clock I decided it was time for some spontaneous silliness and harmless kidding. For some reason, right after that, the conversation slowed down," he explained uncomprehendingly.

It was clear that Irv had overreacted to the book. Apparently he had learned the art of small talk quite well. If his report was accurate, Monique seemed to be enjoying their low-key conversation enormously. Then suddenly he changed gears; he shifted his approach and no doubt confused Monique. Instead of cheering her up he made her a little uncomfortable and she clammed up.

Irv was so enthusiastic about learning to act unshy that he wanted to put every idea to work for him in one evening. That just isn't necessary.

If the mood and atmosphere on a date is comfortable and warm, don't inject new things into it that disturb the continuity. Use whatever works until it doesn't work anymore—only then should you shift gears.

And don't underestimate any of the suggestions in the book. Some of them might strike you as corny or obvious. That may be true, but they are also damned effective. Every idea that's in this book is here because it *will* help a shy person feel more confident in all situations, social or otherwise.

All an idea has to do is plant a seed in your mind. One of the co-authors wrote a book called *How to Pick Up Girls* and has a file full of letters from readers who swear by it. One eighteen-year-old man wrote that a single sentence in the book had changed his life dramatically. He was at a park in his hometown in Colorado. The park had a fountain in the middle with benches around the sides. The young man was sitting on a bench next to an adorable, red-headed girl. Out of the corner of his eye he could see that she was watching the progress of a small spider crawling along the side of the fountain. He wanted to talk to her but sat there nervously, mute and terrified.

Suddenly one line from *How to Pick Up Girls* popped into his head: "When you want to meet a girl, say something, *anything.*" The young man looked at the spider and instantly turned to the girl. "Do you think that spiders sleep?" he blurted out nervously. She looked at him and laughed. An easy conversation followed and he made a date. This young man swears that that one idea at that precise moment in time "changed my whole damn life."

This book is filled with scores of suggestions to help you. By following them you'll see how easy it is to change: A smile here, a hello there, an occasional telephone call, two or three actions on your part can open up a whole new world of people to you. It doesn't matter if you happen to think half of this book is a crock. Use the other half, or put into practice the ideas that strike your fancy. Use all of it, one concept, a paragraph, or even just one sentence. If it feels right let it work for you—it will help!

There's no master plan for curing shyness. Rather you should pick and choose from the smorgasbord of helpful techniques that are offered here. When you find something that feels right, be ruthless and perservering in your use and practice of it. Use whatever works!

40

The Antishyness Diet

YOU'VE HEARD of the Scarsdale Diet, the Atkinson Diet, the Grapefruit Diet, and the Low-Carbohydrate Diet. Follow the instructions carefully, practice the plan faithfully, and in thirty days you will have taken inches off the waist, trimmed pounds off your bottom.

Well, here is the Antishyness Diet. Follow the instructions carefully, practice the plan faithfully, and in thirty days you will have shed your shy, retreating approach to life. You will be confident in your ability to walk into any party or social gathering and approach, charm, and very possibly date anyone in the room. You will have a livelier, more romantic social life. You will have more people to date and love than you ever dreamed possible. You will be able to do anything a nonshy person can do because you will have mastered the art of acting *unshy*. And that's all it takes to have a happier love life.

Just like any weight-loss diet, the Antishyness Diet helps you get rid of something you don't want: fat and shyness, respectively. Like a weight-loss diet, our Diet helps you gain something: confidence, the confidence that will start to give you a good feeling about yourself and allow you to begin a rich, rewarding social life.

Many of the useful exercises described in other chapters will be mentioned in the Diet. You can refer to those specific chapters anytime you need a refresher or reminder of a particular skill. If you're not exactly sure what you're doing at any step along the way, take a minute to reread the related chapter. The Diet will work more quickly and effectively if each step is executed exactly as described.

For some of you the beginning steps are going to seem very easy, even ridiculous. Do them anyway. They were put there for a reason. Some very shy people are not going to think these earlier exercises are simple at all. For them these exercises are going to be challenging, even difficult. And a gratifying success at these simpler levels wil give them the positive reenforcement needed to move on to the more difficult steps.

Always keep in mind that you should never skip a step. Just like with any diet, if you skip a day or sneak a little shyness here and indulge in a little shyness there, suddenly the whole diet goes down the drain. So don't skip steps. If one step seems easy, do it anyway as preparation for the next. And if a step seems too difficult, don't move on until you've mastered it—even if it takes you seven days instead of the prescribed one. Although the Antishyness Diet is designed to last thirty days, some will want to stay on it for two or three times as long. That's okay. There's no need to hurry. The important thing is to do each day's exercise *successfully*. And you'll know when you've been successful. You'll just feel good all over!

The Diet is designed to be more challenging and difficult as you go on. But *do not be discouraged*. You are capable of doing everything that's asked of you. The increase in difficulty is gradual enough so that you are never "overchallenged."

However, the Diet moves along rapidly enough so that some of you will be reaping its fantastic rewards in as little as thirty days.

The one point that must be emphasized about this Diet more than any other, is that you've got to *do* it! You have reached a turning point in your life. Today is the day that you are going to take real, positive, definitive action to begin a more rewarding social life. Most diets offer you the chance to look thin. This Diet offers you the chance to start a new life—a life filled with the warmth of friends and the intimacy of lovers. Does it sound impossible, unreal? It's not. It's very possible and very real. Just start this Diet and stay on it. No more cop outs, no more excuses. You've come this far—don't look back. Forge ahead into new and exciting experiences. Share your life with wonderful people.

Enough talk. If you're ready, so is the Diet. Good luck and good socializing. Incidentally, like every good diet, this one will change your appearance so much that family and friends probably won't recognize you after a month. So be sure to let them know you're on a crash diet . . . the one that can make shy people unshy!

(Note: The Diet has not been broken down into separate sections for males and females. In today's society there is really nothing a man can do socially that a woman can't, including asking someone for a date.)

THE ANTISHYNESS DIET

Before starting the Diet, read over the chapters titled "Stop Dressing Shy," "Desensitizing Your Shyness," "How to Project Positive Body Language," "How to Detect Positive Body Language," "Tuning in to Assertiveness," and "Positive Projection." The fundamentals described in these chapters are ones you should keep in mind and use in *every step* of the Diet. They give you very basic but highly effective pointers in projecting the image of a confident, self-assured person. And what a help that will be when you get to the more difficult levels of the Diet!

DAY 1: MONDAY

Walk up to someone of the *same sex* whom you know and have seen before and say, "Hello." Nothing more, simply "Hello." Do this more than once if you are able to.

DAY 2: TUESDAY

Walk up to someone of the *same sex* whom you know and have seen before. Look at them in the eyes and say, "Hello, how are you?" Continue a conversation as long as you can. Do not have any expectations. Leave when the conversation stops.

DAY 3: WEDNESDAY

Walk up to someone of the *opposite sex* who you know and have seen before and say, "Hello."

DAY 4: THURSDAY

Walk up to someone of the *opposite sex* whom you know and have seen before. Look him (or her) in the eyes and say, "Hello, how are you?" Have no expectations. This is not an invitation for a date. This is simply a greeting.

DAY 5: FRIDAY

Approach someone of the *same sex* whom you know and have seen before and ask advice. This step should proceed much like "The First Step" chapter in the book. Talk only for two minutes. Only if you feel an unusual warmth and understanding from that person should you continue the conversation after the initial two-minute period.

DAY 6: SATURDAY

Walk up to someone of the *opposite sex* whom you know and have seen before and ask advice. This step should proceed exactly like "The First Step" chapter in the book. This is *not* an invitation for a date. Have no expectations and talk only for the required amount of time. Only if you feel an unusual warmth and understanding from that person should you continue the conversation after the initial two-minute period.

DAY 7: SUNDAY

Approach an acquaintance of the *opposite sex* and ask advice. This step should proceed like The First Step chapter in the book.

DAY 8: MONDAY

Approach someone of the *same sex* with a small-talk conversation opener. Using this conversation-opener, talk for about five minutes. If the conversation seems difficult or strained, try it with a different person.

DAY 9: TUESDAY

Approach an *opposite-sex* acquaintance with a small-talk conversation opener. Using this conversation-opener, talk for about five minutes. Do *not* have any expectations for this conversation. This step is designed only to make you feel more confident while talking with members of the opposite sex. It is not a date invitation. Again, if the conversation seems difficult or strained with that person, try it with someone else. Remember, do not go on to the next step until you have completed this one successfully.

DAY 10: WEDNESDAY

Approach an *opposite-sex* person, whom you are interested in. This should be someone whom you would like to get to know better; possibly someone whom you will date at a future time. Using a conversation opener, talk for about five minutes. Again, have no expectations and continue the conversation as long as it is comfortable.

DAY 11: THURSDAY

Use the telephone to call someone of the *same sex*. Make the call in order to ask for some form of advice. You are not required to talk for more than three minutes. This step is designed to give you the confidence to speak on the phone naturally and easily.

DAY 12: FRIDAY

Use the telephone to call an *opposite-sex* acquaintance or someone you are interested in. Again, make the call in order to ask for some form of advice. You are not required to talk for more than three minutes and do not continue the conversation beyond that time if you are feeling very uncomfortable.

DAY 13: SATURDAY

Call a good *same sex* friend, companion, or someone you feel very close to. Arrange to attend any evening social function of your choosing with him or her. There should be at least as many strangers as people you know. Ask one acquaintance *(same sex)* and later one stranger *(same sex)* for some form of advice. Look at his or her eyes and converse for as long as you feel comfortable.

DAY 14: SUNDAY

Again call any good *same-sex* friend or companion whom you feel very close to. Ask him or her to attend any daytime or evening social function of your choice with you. There should be at least as many strangers as people you know. Ask one *opposite-sex* friend and one *opposite-sex* acquaintance in whom you are interested for some form of advice. Converse for as long as you feel comfortable. Have no expectations for this conversation. You are interested only in their advice.

DAY 15: MONDAY

Approach at least two *same-sex* friends or acquaintances at work, school, or wherever. Compliment them on some aspect of his or her appearance, their work, or their interests.

DAY 16: TUESDAY

Approach at least one *opposite-sex* acquaintance or someone you are interested in at work, school, and so on. Compliment her or him on some aspect of his or her appearance.

DAY 17: WEDNESDAY

Call a *same-sex* acquaintance on the telephone. Use any small-talk opener to start a conversation. Continue the conversation for eight to ten minutes.

DAY 18: THURSDAY

Call a *same-sex* friend. Make plans to go to a social function with her or him on *Friday* night. Finalize plans. If that person is unable to make plans, call someone else until you have finalized definite plans for *Friday* evening.

DAY 19: FRIDAY

Attend a social function with *same-sex* friend. Talk to at least one *opposite-sex* stranger using a small-talk opener.

DAY 20: SATURDAY

Call any *same-sex* friend with whom you feel comfortable to make plans for that evening. Arrange to attend a social function with that *same-sex* friend. Talk to at least two *opposite-sex* strangers using small talk. Tell an anecdote or humorous story to a group of at least two people whom you meet.

DAY 21: SUNDAY

Again call or visit a *same-sex* friend or acquaintance. Arrange to have a casual lunch with that *same-sex* acquaintance. Go to a place where there are other single people of both sexes and where you feel comfortable.

DAY 22: MONDAY

Go out for a casual meal (lunch or dinner) by yourself. Go to a place where there are many single *opposite-sex* people. Use small talk to start a conversation with at least two *opposite-sex* people.

DAY 23: TUESDAY

Attend a social function of any kind by yourself. Use small talk to start a conversation with at least one *same-sex* and two *opposite-sex* people. Compliment at least one of the *opposite-sex* persons on some aspect of his or her appearance.

DAY 24: WEDNESDAY

Make phone calls to at least two *same-sex* friends. Use small talk to start a conversation lasting for no less than five minutes. With one of these *same-sex* friends, make plans to attend any social function on Saturday. Finalize plans.

DAY 25: THURSDAY

Call someone of the *opposite sex* whom you are interested in and want to know better. Invite them for a casual date for

Friday night. A male should ask his date to dinner, out for a drink, for a ride in the country, and so on. Avoid movies, theaters, or concerts on this first date—it is hard to have conversation in that type of environment.

Females should invite a man for drinks, hors d'oeuvres, wine and cheese, or dinner if it is practical.

Do not give up if the first call you make doesn't work out. *Try someone else until you have finalized, definite plans for Friday night.* For some reason there is always more pressure and tension put on both people during the proverbial "Saturday-night date." So arrange to have the first date on Friday night.

DAY 26: FRIDAY

Good luck! Relax! Enjoy the date!

DAY 27: SATURDAY

Go out with the *same-sex* friend who you called on Wednesday to a singles social function (disco, bar, restaurant, dance, etc.). Use small talk to start conversation with at least four *opposite-sex* strangers. Compliment at least two of them on some aspect of their appearance.

DAY 28: SUNDAY

Late in the morning, call your Friday-night date. Tell him (or her) you enjoyed the evening (lie if you have to). Ask him to go for a walk in the park, ice cream, coffee, brunch, or any other light, casual meeting. If that doesn't work out, make similar plans for some future date.

DAY 29: MONDAY

Invite an *opposite-sex* acquaintance or someone you're interested in for a casual lunch. The luncheon date affords you the opportunity to get to know someone in a casual, relaxed setting. Neither person feels particularly pressured and neither has any expectations because the "date" will end quite naturally when your lunch breaks are over. Use the luncheon date whenever possible.

DAY 30: TUESDAY

Repeat Diet from Day 23.

If you have followed the Diet carefully you have no doubt had more social success than you had ever dreamed possible. Everyone wants to have dates, go out, have fun, and enjoy the company and friendship of others. It's the people who know how to act unshy that really enjoy great social lives.

No doubt after one month on this Diet you're ready to go out and have a ball. So we'll step inside and let you revel in your happiness.

41

Getting Personal

TAKE A minute to recall the last Warren Beatty or Barbra Streisand movie you saw. Whenever Warren and Barbra seemed alone with their prospective lovers they seemed to know exactly what to say and do to sweep them off their feet.

Warren Beatty doesn't spend weeks with Julie Christie talking about the newspaper headlines or the weather. Barbra doesn't use the precious hours with Ryan O'Neal talking about the rising price of groceries or the new porcelain dishes she just bought. Both of these great screen personalities have a deep instinct for turning small talk into *feeling* talk. In a casual, natural way they know how to get personal, very personal, with their acquaintances.

Of course, it's a heck of a lot easier to get personal when you've got a brilliant scriptwriter thinking up lines for you and a leading lady or man whose surrender is already a part of the plot.

Nevertheless, you can learn a great deal from the snappy, playful dialogue in romantic films. It's adventurous, intimate, and moves from the offhand and casual to the sexy and emotional as surely and powerfully as a steamroller. Come to think of it, it has to. Otherwise, there'd be no romance and that'd be pretty boring. Do you find yourself spending time with your dates discussing the latest book or movie? Do you fill the hours of an evening discussing the weather, food, and other people? As mentioned in an earlier chapter, small talk is fine; in fact, it is preferable on a first date or in the early stages of a relationship. But too much small talk, for too long and too often, can turn people off. The people you date want to be part of a warm, feeling relationship as much as you do. But if all they ever hear from you is a current-events rundown or a weather report, they will begin to feel that you're not really interested in them.

Shy people, unfortunately, often have difficulty moving a relationship from its early ritualized stages—"Tell me about your job"—to an intense personal level—"I think you have very sexy eyes." When they're alone with someone they're attracted to and moments occur that invite a personal, warm gesture, shy people often either don't recognize them as "personal" moments, or they feel so uncomfortable in the intimacy of the moment that they start squirming or freeze up in such a way as to ruin its spontaneity. The result is that many potentially close, long-lasting relationships end right there: You just can't expect people who are looking for romance to remain satisfied for very long with a relationship built on platonic friendship or superficial interaction.

If you are currently seeing someone, or have dated someone more than twice, it is time to get personal. This is not to suggest that you suddenly fill your conversation with lavish, intimate words and gestures. They will probably seem as insincere to the other person as they feel to you. But you should become sensitive to the way a person makes you feel—from that point you can begin to move a relationship to a more personal level.

Perhaps you've been out on a delightful date with a charming guy in your apartment building. As he walks you to your door you wonder if he's going to try to kiss you or invite himself in. Part of you wants to kiss him, to be intimate with him, but as the moment gets closer for you to encourage his advances, your shyness begins to rear its ugly head. What if he doesn't want to kiss me? What if I'll seem too forward? "Thank you for a very pleasant evening, Hank," you say stiffly and slip quickly inside your door. You stand there for a minute, depressed and defeated, wondering how you could have done things differently. Next time you feel you want to be closer with someone but don't know how to go about it, search your inner self (much as you did in the "creative compliment" chapter) for a statement about the way you feel. Try something like, "You know, I really had fun tonight. I enjoyed being with you." Nothing artificial about those words, yet you've moved everything into a more personal sphere. You've conveyed to him that he is more than just someone with whom to pass time.

It is also nice to end your evening by giving your date a kiss. Kissing says you know the person is a sexual being and that you're proud of your own sexuality as well. If you're a shy woman, you should know that a simple kiss is not an invitation for a man to sleep with you, and most men know that. However, if he starts to push more than you've planned for, practice your assertiveness by simply stating, "Good night. We'll get together another time."

Don't wait for a personal gesture from your date if *you* feel that the time is right to get personal. Too many relationships end abruptly because neither person knows how the other is feeling. In confusion, unsure if they're receiving messages of rejection or acceptance, both people feign disinterest. Bang—another good relationship bites the dust!

Getting personal can go beyond gentle gestures. If you're really turned on by someone, tell your date she has a sexy body or sensational legs or a classic profile. You can let her know that you never had such a wonderful meal in your life because you shared it with her. And what would be wrong with letting her (or him) know that you feel the times you spend together are "special."

Consider what's going on in the mind of the person you're dating when you *don't* get personal. You act very sweet, polite, and considerate, but you never give a clear message of how you *feel*. Not knowing that you're shy, the other person begins to have doubts: "He (or she) finds me unattractive. He's gay, married. I have bad breath. She's playing it cool because she doesn't really like me," and so on and so on. Whatever their thoughts, they begin to avoid you to protect themselves from the rejection they believe is inevitable.

Not long ago two good friends, Mike and Virginia, were introduced to each other because they seemed like they would really hit it off. They have many similar interests and though both are shy, once they feel comfortable with people, they are delightful to be around.

A month after their first date Virginia was at a cocktail party alone. When asked about Mike she said that the relationship hadn't worked out. She explained that they went out five times after the first evening, twice to dinner, twice to the theater, and one Saturday they spent the afternoon horseback riding. She said that she had a good time on all the dates and was growing to like Mike a lot. But because she sensed he didn't like her, she felt it was best they didn't see each other again. When asked what made her think Mike didn't like her, she said simply, "In all the times we went out he never tried to kiss me good night. It was like I had rabies or something."

A week later Mike was sitting alone at a local bar looking grim and unhappy. He said that Virginia was the first girl he had ever really liked and he couldn't stop thinking about her. He couldn't understand why she didn't want to see him again. "I wasn't the least bit pushy. Hell, I never even tried to kiss her good night. I guess she just didn't like me," he said and sighed.

You couldn't help but smile at the irony. Here were two shy people, both falling in love, and because they were unable to say how they felt about each other, they were about to let a beautiful experience pass them by. If they had only tried to get personal, they would have realized how much they really felt for one another. Usually it only takes one of the two people involved to begin the process of *getting personal*.

It was a simple task to get Mike and Virginia back together. At first they seemed embarrassed, but soon they were talking like old friends. Over the next few weeks each of them was privately counseled about the importance of "getting personal," how necessary it is to strengthening and improving a relationship. Today, four months later, Mike and Virginia are still dating and apparently getting *very* personal.

The best reason to learn to get personal is to get *really* personal later on. Getting personal is a prelude to a healthy, romantic, and sexual relationship. Woman or man, if you're constantly proper and careful, and never express the good feelings you have for another person, a relationship will rarely rise to its greatest potential.

So start getting personal and expressing how you feel. Don't say to someone, "Would you believe I'm still a virgin?" That's not the right kind of personal talk. Below is a somewhat classic list of personal things to say already compiled for you. As always, it would be better to use something that's spontaneously your own. But until you get the hang of it, feel free to borrow from this list:

GETTING PERSONAL
- I really had a good time tonight.
- I love the way you talk (walk, laugh, smile . . .).
- You're really fun to be with.
- You make me feel good.
- I'm so glad we met.
- You have the greatest eyes.
- I feel very comfortable with you.
- You make me feel very romantic.

- I'd like to see you more often.
- I look forward to our dates. It turns my whole week around.

GETTING MORE PERSONAL
- You have a very sexy body.
- Your perfume really turns me on.
- I'd like to hold you.
- I'd like to kiss you.
- There's something about you that is very sexy.

Notice how all of the "personal" statements include the words "I" or "me." These are just a selection of sayings but all are very effective. If the idea of saying things like the above are entirely unthinkable for you, then it's time to get tough: The truth is, it is impossible to have a continuing, intimate relationship without getting personal. So try it the next time you're with someone special.

42

Keeping Things Sexual

OF ALL the millions of ways to learn about people, to get to know them intimately, to open up to them and share your innermost thoughts with them, sex is by far the best.

It takes more than sex, of course, to build a strong relationship that will last through time, but without sexual relationships with people you care about, you're resigned to a life of platonic friends and one-night stands—a pretty cold and lonely existence.

Shyness should never stop you from having a great sex life. After all, just about everybody—shy or not—likes sex. Wanting to be intimate with another person is one of the strongest instincts people have, and "doin' what comes naturally" is one of the most pleasurable activities on earth. Once you are able to relax in the company of the opposite sex you will be able to rationally consider what you need to do to move things to the physical.

The trick is in *initiating* sex. Every shy person knows the panicky feeling of wanting to get intimate with someone and not knowing how to do it, and the agony of letting the "magic moment"—when going to bed with someone could be accomplished with just a little effort—slip away.

Take Michael, a theatrical electrician on Broadway whose shyness was the only obstacle between him and the thousands of beautiful singers, actresses, and dancers he worked with each day. Michael had more opportunities to meet women than 90 percent of the male population, but he would never go out with a girl unless she practically beat down his door, so he rarely had dates. But at one cast party he attended (he'd only planned to make an appearance and then quickly leave—his usual routine at these functions), a pretty young dancer from the show approached him and started to talk to him. Of course, she was so pretty, so friendly, so likable that Michael started to panic, but she wouldn't let him get away. To make a long story short, the dancer went home with Michael afterward. He couldn't believe it. Here was a girl, a great girl, a gorgeous girl, a girl to dream about, who was sitting in his apartment and who actually seemed fascinated by him!

And Mike was equally fascinated at his own ability to make conversation. They talked with each other for hours.

It seemed that they had everything in common, and a million things to talk about. The clock ticked on. At one forty-five, Michael knew it was do-or-die time. He steeled himself to kiss her, made what seemed to him like a desperate lunge, then retreated immediately afterward. The girl smiled, bewildered, as Michael went back to chatting about his dog and his new records, as though his monumental effort at intimacy had never happened. By two-thirty, the dancer, convinced that Michael wasn't really interested in her, went back to her own place and out of Michael's life forever.

What happened?

Although Michael did overcome his paralyzing shyness for a moment when he kissed the dancer, his move didn't have the timing or follow-through to carry off a successful seduction.

Initiating sex is basically a matter of technique. Nerve has very little to do with it. A shy person with a command of technique will outshine a slick pickup artist every time on the seduction front. Here are a series of specific, concrete things to do to make going to bed with someone for the first time easy, smooth, and pleasurable.

SET UP LOVE VIBES IMMEDIATELY

Out of ignorance Michael succumbed to the single most common pitfall in the art of seduction: waiting too long to get things on a sexual level. By the time he kissed his date, he had built up such a store of anxiety and apprehension that the kiss was little more than a dry, routine motion to get out of the way. Then, once it was over, he went back to talking about nonsexual subjects with which he felt more comfortable.

The secret to enjoying a satisfying sexual encounter is to keep things sexual from the very beginning. As soon as you meet your date, start to set the romance gears in motion. Tell her how great she looks with her hair that way; touch his sweater and let him know how well blue goes with his eyes. These aren't leering remarks that can be misunderstood, just friendly comments designed to put your partner at ease. You may feel your shyness pop up every once in a while, but remember that no one else notices it and be diligent in the use of these techniques to move things to the sexual.

If you have trouble opening a conversation, little compliments can be lifesavers. Is he wearing an unusual ring? Remark on it. Where did the stone come from? There might be an interesting story behind it. Did she make those beautiful earrings she's wearing? Everything a person wears, carries, or treasures is a memento of their interests, their work, or their special experiences in life. Bringing these things to attention not only gives you a wealth of personal conversational material, but lets the person you're with know right from the outset that you're interested in learning about them and getting to know them better.

EASE INTO ROMANCE

Sometimes shy persons will overcompensate for their shyness by "coming on strong"—telling off-color jokes, using street language, or talking about their exploits with former lovers. While this might work to get things on a sexual level, it can be disadvantageous in a new relationship, reducing intimacy in favor of an unromantic sexual performance.

Women, particularly, run the risk of being "used" time and again by men who are only doing what they think is appropriate when they consent to fast sex with a girl who comes on too strong. Ann, a strikingly beautiful blonde who for some deeply buried psychological reason believes herself to be unattractive to men, constantly fails in her attempts to have a long-term relationship, although she makes it clear that she's available. When a man calls her up and says he'd like to see her, Ann's answer is invariably, "Sure. I'll be right over." In her attempts to overcome her basic fear of men, she takes off her clothes and hops into bed with the guy even before he's had a chance to offer her a drink. Then, when he dumps her (usually for a less attractive woman), she can't figure out why, nor can she explain why she never seems to have fun in bed with a man. She has a vague idea that her shyness is in some way to blame, that she gets used because she fears rejection, but she doesn't know what to do about it.

Sex, to be good sex, has to be relaxed, comfortable, and intimate. Take your time approaching it for the first time with a new person, sprinkle in a little romance and a lot of friendliness, and the result will be one of the most pleasurable and memorable experiences of your relationship with your lover.

Allow your shyness to slow your pace, provided it doesn't prevent you from keeping things a little sexual.

IN THE MOOD

Lighting, music, and atmosphere count a lot with turning a prospective lover into a full-fledged bed partner. Be careful that you don't take a date to a setting that reflects your shyness.

If you're taking someone out, the selection of the place where you go is all-important. Make it comfortable, interesting, and, above all, romantic. Is the service good? Will you and your date be treated like special people there? Is the lighting flattering? (You'll look better, and so will your date.) If so, you've found the right spot.

If financial limitations prevent you from going all-out to an elegant, atmospheric restaurant, just do something different or arrange to go to two places during the course of an evening. Start out at a convivial, noisy restaurant or deli for dinner, and then proceed to a quiet, secluded little bar for drinks afterward. A bustling eatery will set a fun tone for the evening, making conversation easier, and the mellow mood of the bar will help with your entree to romance.

A variation of the double-stop date is to do something active during the first part of the evening, and follow it with dinner. Go horseback riding, play tennis, or take a walk around the zoo together. Make sure it's an activity where you'll be able to talk to one another. Movies, concerts, and the theater are more conventional ways to start off an evening, but they don't allow people to get to know each other well, so it's best to save these events for a time when you're already very familiar with your date. When your eye is trained on romance and, eventually, sex, an intimate tete-à-tete is far preferable to a setting where you and your date don't have to exchange a word for hours.

If you're just "trying out" the person you're with, the active daytime double-stop date is perfect. Just invite the person for a couple of hours of fun on the tennis court or at the ice skating rink, and don't mention dinner or drinks until you're sure you want to spend more time with them. If you do, then, when you invite the person for a bite, it will come as a pleasant, spontaneous surprise. And one of the great ways to act unshy is with spontaneous behavior.

If you're inviting someone to dinner at your place, you can control the atmosphere so that it's as romantic as you want it. Keep the lights fairly low (no overhead lights) and augment it with candlelight around the room. Scented candles look nice and give off a romantic fragrance, too. Set the radio to a station that plays music that doesn't inhibit conversation (jazz, "mood" music, or classical stations provide good background music) or have records ready to play. If you're going to play records, though, change them with a minimum of fuss and bother, as each trip to the record player is an interruption in the conversational flow and in the romantic atmosphere.

Make sure everything in your house is comfortable and clean (no newspapers strewn around the floor, no piles of garbage blocking the entrance to the kitchen), but first make sure the bed is made! There's nothing like freshly laundered sheets to make a bed look inviting.

CONVERSATION IS THE KEY

Soft lights, music, elegant drinks, and fancy dinners are all part of a successful seduction, but the most important ingredient in creating a sexy atmosphere is the conversation.

"Date" conversation should *always* be personal in nature. Your job, your politics, your interests are only interesting insofar as they relate to you. Of course, it's easier to make neutral conversation about sports, work, news events, and so on, but that kind of talk won't get you into the more personal aspects of a relationship with anyone. In fact, it will almost surely have the opposite effect. Your date will feel that the things you're saying could be said to a crowd of a thousand, and that you don't feel anything special toward him or her. Also, a two-hour conversation about the devaluation of the dollar doesn't lead smoothly to making love. After a long stretch of neutral conversation, attempts at seduction will seem awkward and contrived.

Stick with you-and-me talk from the beginning. If a neutral subject comes up, personalize it. Blizzard in town? Tell him how your car got stuck in the snow and you had to walk four miles to work to find your place of employment closed. Going to law school? Instead of giving a detailed description of torts, talk about why you decided to study law and what it means to you. Make the conversation and atmosphere more intimate, so, by the time the "date" portion of your evening is over and you two are alone, the conversation should be quite personal.

Once you step through the front door, forget everything except the two of you. Politics and work are meaningless now. News events no longer exist. You have no other acquaintances but the person you're with. You have never been with another man or woman whose company you enjoyed so much. At this point, when things are getting more intimate, you may find yourself getting nervous or even frightened. This is the perfect time to use desensitization (described in a previous chapter) until the nervousness passes.

To zero in on intimate, seductive conversation, begin by keeping all talk centered on the person you're with. Talk about all the good qualities about him or her you've noticed throughout the evening. Ignore any defects, or turn them into compliments. For example, if your date is self-conscious about her weight, comment on how voluptuous she looks. Working to make a person feel comfortable and wanted is an ideal way for a shy person to temporarily pull out of his shyness, so use this technique as often as you can. Giving admiration and confidence to another can do nothing but good, both for a long-term relationship and for the short-term goal of moving.

Tell your date what it was about him or her that attracted you in the first place. Don't be afraid of sounding too intimate or vulnerable. This is the time to act as sensitively as you feel. Let her know that the sparkle in her eyes makes her whole face light up, or that you could pick her walk out of a crowd in Yankee Stadium. Tell him that his smile looks like it comes straight from his heart. Let him know that you appreciate all the trouble he went to to make this evening such a special one for you. Use any of the "getting personal" lines described in the previous chapter.

KISSING

Don't wait until you're alone at home with your date to initiate a first kiss, because it can be awkward, as it was in Michael's case, if you do. Although you may find it difficult to steal a kiss easily in an evening, doing so will both help you get a feeling of what the other person thinks about you and make things easier later on.

Physical contact should be made as early as possible, and carried on throughout the evening. Kiss your date when you say hello. Kiss during dinner. It will be spontaneous, flirtatious, and fun. Since a restaurant is a public place, you won't be initiating a passionate clutch, just a nice little buss to break the touch barrier. Of course, don't do it when it's inappropriate: when the waiter is setting down the chicken capon, or when your date has a mouthful of shish kebab. Do it when you're making eye contact and when you're feeling relaxed.

Kiss again in the taxi on the way home. Hold hands. If it's your apartment you're going to, kiss your date again as soon as you enter, even before you turn the lights on. Make this one a biggie, because it's going to set the tone for what's to follow.

When you offer your date a drink, sit close by, within touching distance. This is the time to begin your nitty-gritty intimate talk with your date—how much fun he was, how lovely she looked during dinner, how much the two of you have in common. No matter how nervous you are at this point, keep your voice close to a whisper (a quiet voice will keep your date physically close to you) and look straight into her or his eyes.

THE PROPOSITION

When the "magic moment" is at hand, you'll both know it. She'll tell you with her eyes; he'll let you know by his touch. Yes, this is the difficult part, but if you've set up the preceding elements of your evening properly, the proposition should come off smoothly.

Be direct but gentle, dignified but sexual, as you invite your lover to bed. Look into his or her eyes and softly say: "Come to bed with me." Or "I want to make love to you." Then take your lover by the hand and escort her or him every step of the way into the bedroom. Do not send your date off alone while you turn off the stereo, clear away the glasses, or roll a joint. It will break the mood if you do. Go in together.

If your first invitation is refused don't go to pieces or beg for forgiveness or end the evening abruptly. Many people, both men and women, need to know that an invitation is serious and won't go to bed before a second or third attempt is made. Just stay cool and continue with personal conversation and intimate gestures. If your date responds with similar intimacy, he or she is undoubtedly turned on and needs only a little prompting to encourage them into bed.

Hang in there. You will succeed.

43

Undercover Work

THE SECRET to good sex is to keep things spontaneous and fun. It's an act of pleasure, after all—not a rigorous discipline requiring exact technique. Everybody's lovemaking is unique. There's no right or wrong way to go about having sex, as long as you enjoy yourself.

But shy people often complain that even when everything goes smoothly and they do end up in bed with someone, their shyness often crawls under the sheets with them. Even shy married people sometimes find themselves inhibited from enjoying sex with their mates because they're unable to relax and let themselves go during lovemaking.

Although there's no one technique to having good sex, here are some pointers designed to eliminate awkwardness and allow you to express yourself more freely in bed.

UNDRESSING

This is the biggest obstacle new lovers face and for shy people it's worse. Taking your clothes off, especially in front of someone who's never seen you naked before, can be nerve-racking. Is my stomach sticking out? How about my skinny legs? Oh, God, my stretch marks! But everybody, the bold as well as the shy, the beautiful and the plain, experiences these same trepidations to some degree with a new lover.

Overcome your nervousness by helping your partner. That is, if you're a man, undressing a woman before making love to her can be one of the most sensual experiences possible. You'll watch her come closer to you, bit by bit, minute by minute, as you take off her defenses along with her clothing.

But *where* to strip is important. To avoid any embarrassment don't attempt to disrobe her on your living room sofa while she's nursing her brandy alexander. You don't want her to feel cheap or silly, so keep this dignified.

Wait until you take her into the bedroom to begin, then start with the smaller items—her bracelet, a scarf, or her shoes. Go slowly. Kiss her neck after you remove a scarf or necklace. Take her shoes off from a kneeling position, and then kiss the inside of her knee. Unbutton her blouse or dress (don't forget the cuff buttons) *slowly*, savoring each new revelation of flesh. Open her clothes and touch her skin, her breasts, her abdomen before taking her garment off.

Compliment her. Remember, she's very nervous now, and wants to be told that you like what you see. "You're so beautiful!" whispered the moment after her dress falls to the floor will set her more at ease than a dozen martinis would.

If she wants to help you undress, let her, but do most of the work yourself. Men's clothing is bulkier, bigger, and more complicated to unfasten than women's, so if you don't give her a hand, she may fumble and get embarrassed.

If you're a woman, help him undress you by taking off your pantyhose quickly and unobtrusively as soon as you can. They're more comfortable than stockings and garters, but, alas, they rate zero in the sex department. There's just something about that zigzag line running from the crotch panel up your abdomen that looks somewhat less than seductive. Also, no man can take them off without confusion and contortions, and he'll feel bad if he pokes a hole in them, which he invariably will. Take them off yourself, and everything will go more smoothly.

If he's very shy himself, and leaves you on your own to get undressed, remove your hose first, then proceed to your other garments down to your bra and panties or slip. Sometimes a scrap of clothing left on is more of a turn-on than complete nudity. When the time comes, he'll take it off for you.

KISS

Once you're both undressed, kiss. It's the most natural thing to do at this point. But kiss like you mean business. Hold her close to you. Wrap your arms lightly around his neck, or touch his face. Kiss on the eyelids, ears, throat, fingers. Kissing keeps things romantic, and lets your lover know you care. You'll probably still be a little nervous now, so don't try to do more than kiss and touch until you're both at ease. In fact . . .

DON'T DO ANYTHING UNTIL YOU'RE READY!

Sex should never be rushed. Your lover, male or female, doesn't want to go to bed with the holder of the world's speed record, so take your time and enjoy every second of every phase of lovemaking. Innocent kissing, done long enough, can turn into hot passion; gentle touching and stroking becomes feverishly sexual if you give it enough time. Don't rush into the next phase before you've exhausted the last. By the time you're ready for the sex act itself, the two of you should practically be panting in anticipation.

KEEP IT STRAIGHT THE FIRST TIME AROUND

If you've never been with your lover before, you don't yet know what he or she likes, so avoid anything too fancy or exotic the first time. Straight sex is easier than variations, so it will keep your Nervousness Quotient low until you get to know each other better. Also, you don't know if your lover is squeamish about doing things you might enjoy, and risking a rejection the first time out is unnecessary. It takes time to become sexually "in tune" with a lover. The more often you go to bed with a person, the freer you'll feel to try new things together. But for now, it's better to leave the tricky moves for later.

LOVE TALK

Silent lovemaking has its thrills, but the most intimate and romantic sex should involve some verbal exchanges. While you're making love, tell your partner how good it feels, how beautiful or strong or tender or soft or sweet your lover is, how much it turns you on, how special your lover is to you, and generally how wonderful it is to feel so close to her or to him. Love talk reduces tension and "performance anxiety" for both partners, and makes you feel that you're having sex *with* someone, not *for* them.

Talking "dirty," too, is a definite turn-on during lovemaking, although many people are supershy about using explicit language. But it's worth the risk, if you just force yourself to get the words out of your mouth. Tell your woman how much you love to fuck her, or tell your man how hot and hard his cock is, and watch the response. Sex talk is all part of the game of acting unshy. Lovemaking is a very private thing, and even the straightest lover won't think less of you for using a few choice words at the right moment.

AIM TO PLEASE

Let your lover know you care about their satisfaction. If your partner asks for something, or indicates through his or her responses that something you're doing is a special turn-on, try to give it. Moreover, when you give it, give it all the way. Sex takes time to build to fever pitch, so a mere token of what your partner likes won't do the trick. If she likes you to fondle her breasts, keep it up, just the way she likes it, for as long as it takes. If he likes his penis squeezed, do it with a regular rhythm until he tells you to stop. Repetition in sex is not boring. It's just the opposite. The longer you do something in the same rhythm, the more exciting it becomes. A hundred different kinds of caresses all over the body won't be as sexually stimulating as one pleasurable movement repeated regularly for a lengthy interval.

FANTASIZE

Everybody has bedroom fantasies while making love. Sometimes they're verbal, sometimes visual, or both. There's nothing perverted about imagining that the person you're with is someone else, or imagining that you yourself are a movie star or sex symbol. In fact, psychologists say that often this kind of identity swapping permits people to have some of the most abandoned and relaxed sex they've ever experienced.

Why not try it? The next time you're in bed with someone, picture yourself not as yourself, but as Cary Grant, Napoleon, Jane Russell—whoever you think of as sexy, confident, and relaxed in their lovemaking. Do whatever the person of your fantasies would do. Allow yourself to fill in every nuance of the role with your hands, your body, your speech. Maybe *you* might never be able to bring yourself to tell a girl to spread her legs, but Jack Nicholson might!

Your mind is your own private place where you can do *anything* you want. While you're making love, let the images and words that drift into your consciousness remain there. Explore them. Enjoy them. Nobody is going to chastise you for enjoying your own thoughts.

Sex is meant to be naughty—that's the fun of it! Let your imagination go where it wants to go, and each time you have sex will be a totally different, totally *hot* experience.

TAKE AS MUCH AS YOU GIVE

Remember, your partner wants to please you too. The two of you are together because you both have the same feelings about each other, so be as intimate, cuddly, and *taking* as you want.

Just as Juliet told Romeo, "The more I give to thee, the more I have, for both are infinite," the more pleasure you accept from your lover, the better it will be for both of you. The shy man is often so much of a giver that he becomes too anxious about pleasing his partner to derive maximum pleasure himself. He worries about whether or not he's exciting his lover properly, or if his moves are gentle or forceful or imaginative enough. Such caring is a wonderful quality, but sex is the one occasion where a certain amount of selfishness won't take away from the total effect. In bed, you and your lover are both sex objects, so you might as well enjoy yourself. Allow yourself to be handled and fondled and loved. Allow yourself to take your lover and enjoy yourself with him or her. Allow yourself to have fun taking sex and being taken.

Even allow yourself to come first, if that's how things work out. Rarely do two people have climaxes at the same time, and almost never when the lovers aren't very experienced with one another, so there's nothing wrong with coming ahead of your lover as long as you see that your partner is taken care of eventually.

In short, whatever you and your lover want to do—do it. Sextime is *your* time, and there are no rules or restrictions you have to observe, no facades you have to keep up. Once you're in bed with a lover, you're no longer the Great White Hunter, the Poor Girl Alone, or any other role you give yourself to function in society. You're just a natural man or a real woman with your lover, doing what men and women have been doing since the beginning of time. If you remember that what you're doing is absolutely normal and natural, your lovemaking is bound to become freer, more relaxed, and infinitely more satisfying.

44

The Morning After

WHAT COULD be a more beautiful sight than to wake up in the morning and find the person you've made love with for the first time the night before sleeping next to you?

Unfortunately, all too often shy people wake up after a night of close contact, intimacy, and lovemaking to find themselves naked, both literally and figuratively. The beauty and magic of the past evening seems to disappear, and the shy person is left with a thousand fears of what to do and say. The ease and spontaneity of last night is replaced by awkwardness and silence; the closeness gives way to a terrifying distance.

If you've experienced a bummer of a morning after, don't dread the next time you'll be waking up with someone new. It doesn't have to be a time of reversion to strangerhood. In fact, with a little knowledge and understanding, the morning after can be as loving and exciting as the night before.

First, bear in mind that a certain awkwardness is only natural, even for self-assured people. After all, at least one of you is waking up in a strange place, in strange surroundings, and with someone who—until the night before—was almost a stranger.

It's not easy to trust somebody, especially someone who has explored every inch of your body without necessarily knowing some basic things about you. You suddenly feel indignant that the man who said those things to you last night doesn't even know how many brothers and sisters you have, or that the girl who elicited that animal response from you never heard of your uncle the Mafia Don.

It's *normal* to feel anxious, strained—even a little disappointed—the next morning. It took a lot of time, effort, and magic to achieve the perfect communion of the night before. It was a new experience, and a successful one. Well, the next day is a new experience too, and like all new experiences, it can be uncomfortable at first (remember how nervous you were the moment before you said, "I want to make love to you?"), but can grow into something beautiful. Just as the warm, loving feeling of the night before can be repeated over and over, every day will get better as you learn more about your new lover.

Take the initiative to turn the morning after into a wonderful experience and see how quickly you and your lover get back into the same intimate feeling of the night before.

Let your lover know how special he or she was and still is. Kiss her awake. Talk to him—about how nice he looks when he's sleeping, about how you woke up in the middle of the night, relieved and delighted to see his face on the pillow next to you. Bring her coffee in bed, before breakfast. Keep in mind that this is your *lover*—this morning as well as last night—and that, as such, she or he rates the best of your attentions.

Spend time in bed together. If you have to rush out in the morning, set the alarm extra early so you can spend some time with your lover before jumping into the shower. Making love in the morning is probably the best way to rekindle the magic of the night before, plus it starts you off on a terrific day!

Know when to leave. If you're the visitor at your lover's house, leave early enough so that he or she can get dressed and moving without disrupting a normal morning routine. Your lover may feel awkward dressing with you waiting in the wings, or might feel compelled to keep you entertained. If you've got to go, go. Do it tenderly and with lots of kissing and hugging, but make it fast and unobtrusive.

Be a good host or hostess. If it's your home, keep your refrigerator stocked with orange juice, coffee, milk, and a few frozen Danish to offer your lover. He or she may not be able to leave before you do, so a little breakfast can keep your lover occupied while you go through your normal motions.

Also, in your home, give your visitor time to pull him or herself together. Your lover doesn't want to impose on you, and might not ask for use of the bathroom or shower—might even be embarrassed about getting dressed in front of you—so allow her or him some time alone. Clear out of the bathroom as soon as possible and go make coffee or buy a paper. If you're accustomed to putting on your makeup or drying your hair in front of the bathroom mirror, move your equipment elsewhere for the moment so that your lover doesn't feel he or she needs to wait in line to wash up.

See that your lover gets home safely. It's good form for a man to see a woman who's spent the night with him home. If you can't take her home yourself, don't relegate her to the bus or subway after she leaves you—it might make her feel cheap. Instead, send her home in a taxi, and pay the driver ahead of time. Tell her you'll call her soon. When you say good-bye give her a soft little kiss on the lips or on the cheek, and a squeeze of her hand to let her know that you're still the same fantastic guy you were the night before.

A woman doesn't have to take uch pains with a man who's leaving, but do make him feel wanted and appreciated. Tell him you'll never forget the wonderful night you spent together. And no matter how tired you are when he goes, smile, take him to the door, and kiss him good-bye.

Have a morning date. If you're both not hurrying off to work, one of the nicest things to do on the morning after is to go out to breakfast together. Breakfast is the one meal that's not expensive no matter where you go, so choose the most elegant, ritzy place around. Hotel dining rooms are good breakfast spots, and sometimes good restaurants are open for breakfast or brunch on weekends. Eating breakfast out also means no cooking, no dishwashing, and no distractions. All you have to concentrate on is each other. At an elegant breakfast out you can pick up on the morning after right where you left off the night before.

Don't arrange the next date immediately. Unless your lover asks for another date during the course of your evening and morning together, don't bring up the subject then. Much of the beauty of romance lies in its spontaneity, so you don't want to convey the impression that you're a clinger. Just tell your lover that you want to see him or her again soon, and that you'll call. It will leave a little mystery to your beautiful encounter, and when you do call, it will be that much more appreciated.

Try calling just to say hello. A thoughtful morning-after touch is to call your lover the same day you leave one another. It can be as soon as you get home or later on, but a call from a lover of the night before is always welcome. Say, "I just wanted to hear your voice again," or "You were so wonderful, I wanted to make sure I didn't make you up." Keep the call short and sweet—a little reminder that you remember and care.

Getting really intimate with someone only begins when you first go to bed together, and gets better and better every day. Be good to your lover by the cold light of dawn as well as by the flicker of candlelight, and you can be sure she or he will come back for more! Your shyness doesn't have to keep you from enjoying the pleasures of a gratifying sexual experience.

45

Continuing a Relationship

CALLING FOR the second or third date is easier than initiating a relationship with someone, but it can still be a sticky proposition. Those shyness demands have been at work on you for a long time, and it's hard to be confident that someone wants to see you again, even if he or she seemed to have a great time with you before.

But continuing a relationship, like beginning one, requires only 1 percent nerve and 99 percent technique. Knowing what to do and say will keep any residual nervousness to a bare minimum, and will eliminate any awkwardness that might spring from getting together with someone after that first encounter.

CALL BACK PROMPTLY

When you want to invite your lover to see you a second time, don't wait too long after the first encounter to call again. While you don't want to press your date into a heavy commitment on your first time out, you also don't want to let time erase the beauty and specialness of your first night together.

Two or three days after your first date is a good interval. Your lover will still be thinking about you, but will have had enough time to miss you, too.

Even if you didn't have sex with your date the last time you were together, it's a good idea to wait a couple of days to let the love vibes build up between you.

OPEN THE CONVERSATION EASILY

To avoid those uncomfortable first moments on the phone when you don't want to blurt out your invitation immediately but can't think of anything else to say, open the conversation with a specific reminder of the last time you were together. If she bumped her head getting into the taxi, you can ask her if it's still bothering her. If he left on a business trip after your last encounter, ask him about the city he visited. Or bring up an experience that the two of you shared. If you had a Pina Colada for the first time with your date, mention that you've been whipping them up in your blender ever since.

Your opening comment should be specifically related to your lover, not a bland "how ya doing?" or "how's the job?" Zero in on a specific incident or exchange which was meaningful enough for both of you to remember. It will give you an easy way to start the conversational ball rolling, and—more importantly— it will show your lover that your last time together was special and memorable to you.

USE COMPLIMENTS GENEROUSLY

Your lover or date isn't a stranger anymore, so let yourself be a little romantic, even over the phone. Say something like, "I've been thinking about you all day," or "Ever since last Tuesday, I've been on a great high." Your lover will love to hear it, and it'll bring back the closeness of your last encounter with just a few words.

In fact, the conversation leading up to a second invitation needn't be much more than a stream of gentle mutual compliments. You don't have to resort to talking about the weather, and you don't yet know your lover well enough to discourse on any pressing problems in your life, so enjoy some lighthearted lover's talk that will make you both feel good. Tell her how pretty she looked—"I wish I'd had a camera to take a picture of you on the Ferris wheel with the sun behind you"—or how much you enjoyed your conversation—"I went home and thought about what you said. It really made me think."

Talking on the telephone is often easier for shy people than eyeball-to-eyeball confrontations so learn to use this valuable tool in your love relationships. Use the telephone tips from a previous chapter if the phone still gives problems.

Even when you're not calling for a date, a friendly chat on the phone will let your lover know you're thinking about him or her, and will also allow you a way to get to know each other with almost no anxiety.

BE DIRECT

When asking for a date the direct approach works best. When the time is right, come right out and ask, "Would you like to see me again?" Your lover's yes will make the rest of the conversation easy.

SAMPLE CONVERSATION:

"Would you like to see me again, Claudia?"
"Sure."
"Great. How about Thursday?"

"Okay. What do you have in mind?"
"I'd like to see the Arts Festival downtown. Want to go?"

or

"I'd like to make dinner at my house."

or

"Well, I've declared this Thursday to be National Claudia Day, and I think we ought to celebrate."

Asking if your date would like to see you again is much less complicated than inquiring if she or he is "busy" on Thursday. Your lover might indeed be busy, but may want to see you all the same. However, the answer, "Yes, I'm busy" is usually interpreted by shy people to mean, "No, I don't want to see you," even though that may be far from the truth. Better to come right to the point and find out if your lover is willing before getting to particulars of the evening you have in mind.

GO SOMEWHERE DIFFERENT

If you went out for dinner and drinks the first time out, change the program a little for the second date. Invite your lover for a party, a day at the races, a home-cooked meal—or whatever, so long as it's different from your previous activity. Doing something new together will give the two of you a whole new set of experiences to share, a new bank of memories to tap later. Also, repeating the same activity that brought you so close together before may be a disappointment the second time around. The amusement park that seemed so much fun on your first date could seem inexplicably boring and childish when revisited; the romantic ride on the ferryboat might not be repeatable.

And don't go near the same restaurant you went to for at least another month! *That* conversation was too special to make a successful rerun, and an attempt at recapturing a wonderful time in the same place is bound to pale beside the glorious memory of it all, leading you both to mistakenly believe that either the thrill is gone or that your terrific first encounter was just a fluke in an inevitably commonplace relationship.

To keep your love vibes strong, charge them with new experiences built together. Even a bad experience, when shared, can be fun to remember. So what if the next restaurant you go to features surly waiters, a weird clientele, and a menu straight from the Salvation Army soup kitchen? It will still give you a lot to talk about later.

Building a relationship is like building a house. One experience goes on top of another until you have four solid walls of shared times that belong to only the two of you. And if those "bricks" of time spent together are varied and rich and memorable, then the structure of your relationship will be strong enough to protect you from anything that may threaten to come between you.

RECIPROCATE

If you stayed at her house the last time, invite her to spend the night at yours on the next date. Even if you don't feel that your place is as attractive or comfortable as your lover's, she'll want to see where and how you live. Sharing your home with someone, even temporarily, is almost as intimate as sharing your body. If you did the hosting the last time, you can suggest staying at your lover's place, but don't make a fuss if she or he declines. The place may not be in condition for company, or your lover may not have enough food or spirits on hand to feel comfortable with an overnight guest.

Also, if one of you lives with a roommate or with family, the partner with an apartment or house to himself should accept the responsibility for all overnight hosting. The other partner can reciprocate by cooking or washing dishes, bringing liquor or food, or offering to help clean the place.

REPEAT THE SEDUCTION PROCESS EACH TIME

Taking your lover to bed gets progressively easier each time you do it, but the process of seduction has to be reinitiated each time. Even married couples find ways to keep seducing their mates for sexual encounters through the years to keep their sexual relationship lively and interesting.

Never assume that your lover will go to bed with you again just because he or she did so before. You may end up frustrated and confused, wondering why the magic wore off so fast! George and Claire, happily married now, almost didn't make it through their second major encounter. It seems that George, so relieved that the anxiety of wondering whether or not Claire would ever go to bed with him was finally dispelled, walked into her apartment rubbing his hands together and announced: "Hi! Should we eat first or fuck first?"

The little attentions lovers give one another aren't just silly games to pass the time. Each kiss, each gentle word is a declaration that your lover is important to you. Also, all those little hugs and squeezes, built up over a couple of hours, create the kind of sexual tension that, when released, makes for powerful and satisfying lovemaking. And you'll find that feelings of shyness become less and less frequent as you get closer and more intimate.

Each sexual encounter is as new and as special an event as the first, and each should be handled with care. Besides, nobody wants ordinary sex. Make it extraordinary every time with a full-fledged seduction, and you'll both benefit.

BEWARE THE SELF-DESTRUCT TAPE!

Many shy people have a complex, built-in mechanism for screwing up even the most promising relationships. It's as though a little demon inside is doing everything he can to keep the shy person alone and unloved.

And these demons can be subtle. Few shy people are as blatantly self-destructive as Ann, whose promiscuity—which she told herself would win her a good relationship with a man—undermined her chances to be loved and respected. Most of the time the demons disguise themselves as your thoughts, although if you thought about them objectively you'd recognize these ideas for the subversive, "I-Hate-Myself" robot tapes they really are. Here are a few:

Tape No. 1: "She's not really pretty." Okay, your new girlfriend isn't Farrah Fawcett. But neither is Farrah herself once she's out of the TV studios! If you wait for the most gorgeous girl (or guy) you've ever laid eyes on to appear before you extend yourself and offer to share your heart and body, chances are pretty good you'll be disappointed. Even if that angel from heaven does come around, she or he may not have the other qualities your new lover possesses. That laugh of hers or the way he looks at your sketchbook is *worth* something. Sometimes a diamond passes as an ordinary stone for centuries before it's discovered by someone with an eye that sees things a little differently. And that person is amply rewarded in the end by the value of the find.

Tape No. 2: "It's only physical." Remember, it takes a lot longer to understand someone's mind than it does to get acquainted with his or her body. People are complicated creatures, often misrepresenting their true feelings and motivations in favor of what they may think is a more acceptable or "safer" mode of behavior when they first start to see someone. In other words, give your new lover a chance before dismissing him or her as a "cheap trick." You may be surprised at the tender guy underneath the rough facade or of the warm, loving woman waiting to come out of a quiet, girlish shell.

Tape No. 3: "He's (she's) not what I'm looking for." Anyone who plans out every detail of his (or her) great love-to-be before ever meeting him is programmed to self-destruct lovewise. Does the dream lover exist? (What would that perfect man look like in the morning? How would that dream lady ask for a bank loan?) If you haven't got an absolutely accurate character portrait of who you want (and who does?), then more than likely you're creating a half-baked character whose only function is to turn you away from *real* lovers. Or, your insistence on certain attributes in every lover you meet could be satisfying unhealthy needs. Do you really want someone who is never jealous, or will you feel uncared for in the end with such a person? Is it so important to go to bed with only strong, dominating men? Couldn't one of those eventually wreck your own confidence?

Be wary of self-made stereotypes. It doesn't really matter if your new flame talks loud or giggles, does it? You're getting a total package here, a whole human being—not a department-store mannequin molded to your specifications. Differences between people is what keeps us interesting, so if you accept your new lover, warts and all, you may find that he or she *is* what you were looking for all along, without knowing it!

Tape No. 4: "I don't think he/she will make a good wife/ husband/father/mother." Unfortunately—or fortunately, in some cases—not every relationship you have will be an eternal one. If you think too far ahead, you may put a damper on what could otherwise be an enjoyable, growing, or even lasting experience. You and your lover may never marry; you just have to accept that fact from the beginning. You may not get along after three weeks. Or you may hit it off so smashingly that your entire outlook on marriage and parenthood may change. The future is too far away to control or fear, especially where romance is concerned, so concentrate on having a good time in the present, and you'll have nothing to regret later, no matter what happens.

Tape No. 5: "If he/she likes me, there's got to be something wrong with him/her." This is the biggest killer among the demon tapes, and the one poisonous thought behind most self-destructive impulses concerning lovers. It's what prompts you to fall in love with people who hurt you, and fall out of love with people who are good for you. The shy person must constantly fight against his or her own feelings of unworthiness and unlovableness if he or she is ever going to be happy with another person.

Start by not questioning what your lover sees in you. She or he has a network of senses and thoughts that are different from your own, so even if you don't see what you have to offer, accept the fact that your lover does.

Then, don't look for faults. The big ones will emerge all by themselves, and nobody's perfect, so it's pointless and defeating to agonize over every tiny flaw.

Finally, let yourself be happy. You may not think you deserve this lover, but that's just a demon tape playing its tired old song again. If you weren't as great as your lover thinks you are, you wouldn't be together.

Continuing a relationship may seem like the hardest thing in the world to do, but it's also the most rewarding. And with a little effort and a lot of understanding, a budding romance can blossom into one of the greatest and most spectacularly enjoyable experiences of your life. Your shyness simply does not have to prevent you from having fairy tale romances. And the intimacy of a close relationship may be just what the doctor ordered for bringing you out of your shyness shell.

46

The Year of the Shy Person

A MAN sits reading a book on a park bench on a balmy spring afternoon. A few minutes later a jogger in track shorts and T-shirt plops herself down on the same bench. As she's catching her breath, the man comments on what a nice day it is, directing his remark as much to the world at large as to his fellow bench sitter. A few minutes more pass. Sighing peacefully, the woman responds, "Yes, it is a lovely day. Just what we needed. Winter was awful." She too addresses the trees and grass and clouds and frisbee chasers as well as the man reading the book at the end of the bench.

After a bit, the woman asks the man what he's reading. "Hemingway," he says. The woman is intrigued. She tells him Hemingway is her favorite author. The man likes that. "Mine, too," he answers. The conversation is low key, light, intermittent.

Talk turns to other subjects. "What do you do?" "Where do you live?" "How far do you jog every week?" Before long an hour has passed. The woman says she has to go now. The man offers to accompany her through the park. "I'd like that," she remarks. They stroll past the duck pond and laugh as a young child talks to the ducks as if they were his nursery-school classmates.

At the edge of the park is an art museum. The woman mentions it contains some of her favorite paintings. The man asks her to show them to him. The woman checks her watch. What the heck, she thinks. Why not? The couple spends an hour or so wandering around the cool quiet halls of the Contemporary Painters wing, then has coffee in the museum cafeteria.

As they sip espresso, the man mentions he is planning to see a new Woody Allen film tonight. The woman's eyes grow wide. Oh, she's dying to see it herself. "Why don't you come along?" the man suggests. "Gee, that'd be nice," the woman responds.

After the movie the man walks the woman back to her apartment. She invites him in and puts on a Jackson Browne album. The man likes that. Jackson Browne is his favorite musician. The woman opens a bottle of good red wine and turns down the lights. The couple sips the Bordeaux slowly, languidly. They are at peace with the world. When the album is through and the wine bottle empty, they reach out and touch one another. The woman then takes the man's hand and leads him into her bedroom.

Do you know something? Twenty years ago this little scenario may never have taken place. Today it happens all the time and is probably unfolding in Kansas City and San Francisco and Chicago and Becket, Massachusetts at this very moment. Who knows, the man and woman on the bench may have been as shy as you, perhaps even shyer. No matter, today it's so easy to meet. People no longer seem willing to let outmoded social conventions stand in the way of their happiness and pleasure, of their getting together. Life is too short, love too much fun. People seem to have lost their appetite for elaborate mating rituals, formal courtships, endless engagements, for living for the future. And that couldn't be better for shy people. For the fact is there are thousands of strangers out there right now just dying to make your acquaintance . . . even if you're shy and awkward and ill-at-ease . . . even if you think you don't stand a chance.

This book has tried to arm you with dozens of practical, easy-to-understand, easy-to-execute techniques for acting unshy. This is all it takes for shy people to find love. Take the man on the bench, for example. Or the woman. Their romance began so easily, so naturally. And all it took was the woman sitting down or the man's first remark. These are the kind of actions you should take. It's the utterance of a simple hello. It's placing yourself close enough to another for nature to take its course.

In most cases shyness is no more than the ten or fifteen awkward minutes it takes to start to get to know someone. As soon as a conversation is underway, gains a little momentum of its own, the shyness often disappears without either party realizing it.

Some shy people think there is something deeply, seriously wrong in their psyches. In a few rare instances this is true. But for the more than eighty million other shy folks in America, even those who think of themselves as dreadfully shy, shyness is often no more than a simple learned response, like spreading a napkin on your lap as you sit down to a meal. It can be unlearned as methodically and scientifically as one unlearns an awkward ballet technique, a poor golf swing.

There are all kinds of emotional exercises you could have been directed through in this book. You could ask yourself, what's the worst that could happen? How shy am I? What kind of shyness do I suffer from? But this would have probably been counterproductive. For where else would you have done your analysis and contemplation but alone in your room? And to what end? It's nearly impossible for a shy person to work through a social problem while sitting deep in thought alone.

Countless shy people, however, have found love and romance by getting out of the house and associating with others. A hello, a smile, a handshake, a nod, a wink—any one of these tiny little pieces of communication can help a shy person get better in an instant. All the soul-searching in the world cannot equal the power of a new person telling you, "You're nice." And that, too, isn't going to happen to you while you're sitting by yourself in your room.

So, go out into the world. Even when you don't feel like it. Make small talk. Be visible to your fellow men and women. Compliment people. Ask them advice. Sit down next to them on planes and buses and trains. Call them on the telephone. Touch them on the arm. Smile at them. Look them in the eye. Listen to them. These are the techniques that will help you connect with others faster and with less complications than you ever dreamed possible. All it takes is for one person to respond positively to you to send your shy behavior on its way. And the really nice thing about that is that it almost never comes back.

You see, once you learn how to connect with other people you never forget. It's like learning how to swim or ride a bicycle. If one relationship ends, you'll know exactly how to jump right back into the fray and find another.

The lion has had its year. So has the sheep and the tiger and the wolf. Now it's time for shy people to come into their own. It's just too easy not to. Thousands of people are out there just dying to meet you, hug you, kiss you, and love you. Don't disappoint them. Just put one or three or a dozen of the antishyness techniques to work and before you know it you'll have the love you've been dreaming about. It can happen this year. With a little bit of luck and courage on your part, it can even happen today.